Loved My Time At Hahn

Memories From a Former Day

©Dr. James E. Martin, MSgt
USAF, Retired

ISBN:

13: 978-1503303850

10: 1503303853

Introduction

Welcome to Hahn Air Base!

If you are like me, prior to my introduction to this neat little place in western Germany in October, 1966, you have probably never heard of it. I will never forget my first knowledge of anything relating to Hahn. I will mention in the lines to follow a few of the details regarding this experience. My memories will be placed after this introduction and will be followed by many others which will be found according to the alphabetical listing.

Many former "Hahnites" have contributed their memories (both good and bad) and these will be included here. **All entries will be listed** alphabetically by last name at the conclusion of my story. Articles will be published as submitted unless there was very obvious spelling or grammatical errors, in which case I have taken the liberty to make corrections.

Entries that are written in the first person are written as submitted. Those that are written in the third person are written from a compilation of material submitted by the contributor in a survey that was posted on Facebook.

I have also included a few pictures which are found sporadically placed among the various contributors, as well as at the end of the book. I am sure these pictures, along with the testimonials will bring back many fond memories and cause great satisfaction as you recall your days from long ago.

Some of the information that various contributors have submitted is very brief and general. Some others have shared very detailed information. Most of the contributors are folks that I have never had the privilege of personally meeting but have only met through e-mail and social media sites.

I put together a very simple survey and many responded in this way. I am very thankful to each one who shared their memories and hope that it will be as interesting to you the reader as it was to me as I have compiled this book in a very simple and readable format.

There have been histories written about the formation, occupancy, and demise of Hahn Air Base. This has always been very enjoyable and informative. My purpose here is not to rehash the historical information, which I would highly recommend that you explore if you have never done so. My purpose herein, as stated previously, is to put together in a very readable format memories that many have retained - some of us for very many years now. It is enjoyable to most of us to read of these memories that others have and compare notes.

So sit back and enjoy as we travel back in time and reminisce about a wonderful time in life. It is very difficult for me to realize that my days at Hahn are as distant as they actually are (I left there in 1969).

I mentioned earlier that many of the submissions are very general and brief. You will notice some redundancy as you read through these many testimonials. This confirms to me a very basic idea regarding the years, from differing decades, that we all spent at Hahn. The simple truth is that we all enjoyed some of the same things and found some of the same things unenjoyable. I feel confident that you will also relate to many of these experiences as you reflect on your time at Hahn.

HAHN AIR BASE

Dr. James E. Martin, MSgt.
USAF Retired

Honored to have been there as a
first assignment,

A youngster with much to learn.

Hearing new sounds we were not
accustomed to,

New tasks we learned to not
spurn.

A memory now that its days are
done,

Is renewed as much older we
become.

Remembering those days again
and   again
And all of the continual fun.

Barely forty plus years since
 departure from its gates

And thankful still for the time.

Sorry that it now remains but a
 memory

Etched forever in my aging mind

My Story:

Martin, Dr. James E.

The year was 1966. Living in Birmingham, Alabama, I was attending a junior college in the area. I had graduated from high school in 1964, and thought I had my life and future plans all figured out.

School progress was only mediocre, at best. I was attending regularly, but my efforts in studies were not really even close to what they should have been. It is amazing how differently things are when observed from a much more mature perspective.

To better understand the dangers of this situation, try to remember some of the other things that were going on at the time. Probably the most significant of these was the war in Viet Nam. By 1966, things were going pretty hot and heavy. It was an exciting time indeed.

I had registered months before this at my local draft board and had been given a school deferment, but I knew that my grades were not sufficient enough to allow this to continue much longer. Worries of being drafted were weighing pretty heavy on my mind. Thoughts of going into the Army and, most likely, being sent directly to Viet Nam were not very pleasant thoughts at that time.

A friend of mine was also attending classes with me and was in a similar situation. Together we came up with what we thought was the perfect solution to the problem. We decided that to avoid being drafted, and to be able to have the ability to choose which branch of service we wished to serve in, it would be in our best interest to consider enlisting. We both agreed that the best of all possible choices was the U S Air Force. So, within a few days we were off to talk to the Air Force recruiter.

The recruiter was a very interesting fellow. He had the unique ability to convince us that we could have everything we wished by signing on the dotted line. We immediately began the process of taking the ASVAB test to determine what we were best suited to do, if we went through with plans to enlist.

To make a long story short, we completed the tests and discovered that we were both best suited to go into the mechanical career field. I decided that I wanted to be an engine mechanic so that I could possibly more easily land a good paying job after the Air Force. I was told that the only thing he could guarantee was the field and not a specific job within that field.

The next step in the process was to get a physical examination to see if we were physically fit for military service. We were scheduled within a few days to accomplish this and we both found that we were indeed physically fit. When the recruiter received this news he was ready to sign us up and have us on our way to basic training.

It was at about this time that I began to realize that we were not quite as ready to leave as the recruiter was to send us off. He began to sense the anxiety and suggested that we enlist under the buddy plan and defer our departure unto a later date. We decided that we would complete the current quarter at school and plan on leaving then. This would give us the necessary time we felt that we needed to say goodbye to family, girlfriends, etc. So this is what we did. We were scheduled to depart for basic training on 17 April 1966.

It seemed like no time at all and it was time to depart. Saying goodbye was not nearly as easy as one might think. It was something, however, that had to be done.

We boarded a bus in route to Montgomery, Alabama, where we finished some final paperwork. Then, we boarded an airplane on our way to San Antonio, Texas, home of Lackland Air Force Base and the rest is, as they say, history. It may be hard to believe, but this was my very first experience of flying on an airplane.

Arrival at Lackland began the experiences that forever changed my life. Much could be said here regarding my stay there, but I will refrain at this time.

It was while at Lackland that we were told that we were going to be going into the Weapons Loading (462x0) career field. I thought to myself (in reference to being able to get a job afterwards) "What airline is going to hire a bomb loader?" I thought at the time that this was a poor decision, but learned later that it was not really that bad of a choice. I actually enjoyed the many years that I served in this capacity.

We soon completed all of the wonderful activities at Lackland and were on our way to Lowery AFB in Denver, Colorado, for technical training on Weapons and Weapons systems. The training was great. I actually had the honor of returning to Lowery as a Weapons Instructor many years later in my career.

It was while at Lowery that we first heard of Hahn Air Base. Several weeks before our graduation date we received orders assigning us to this place that very few had ever heard of.

We were assigned to the 10th Tactical Fighter Squadron which is part of the 50th Tactical Fighter Wing. To a young kid who had hardly been out of the state of Alabama, the prospect sounded great.

After graduation, we returned home for a thirty - day leave and in October, 1966, we boarded a plane in Birmingham. After a long series of tearful goodbyes, we were finally off to the other side of the world to begin what was to be a three - year assignment. To say that this was the first of many very memorable moments in life would be a huge understatement. I will go to my grave with many wonderful memories for which I am extremely thankful.

Arriving in Frankfurt in October, 1966, was a very interesting experience. We were concerned with how we would be able to communicate with folks at the airport since we knew nothing of the German language. Concerns regarding whether anyone would be there to meet us were also present. Needless to say, all concerns were gone once we got inside the Rhein Main facility.

A young man from West Virginia, named A1C Ron Cunningham had ridden the "Blue Goose" to meet us. He was a loader from the 10th Loading Section. On the four hour ride from Frankfurt to Hahn he busied himself with filling us all in on his vast knowledge of Hahn. He talked most of the entire time.

Arrival at Hahn

After an otherwise uneventful ride

(other than observing the cold, foggy drizzle and beautiful scenery) we finally arrived at the front gate to the base. After being cleared by security, we were dropped off at the barracks which was to be home for the immediate future. We were assigned to our rooms and told to be out front the next morning to go to the Loading Section where we would be working.

We soon got "settled" in and crashed for some long awaited rest. The next morning arrived almost instantaneously and we were bussed to the shop. Besides my friend, with whom I had enlisted, there were actually several of us that had been together in tech school. Friendships that had begun there were allowed to continue for quite a while. Once inside the shop and after the usual greetings, etc., we were introduced to which load crew we were assigned and met our load crew chief. I was assigned to load later Sgt) Ed Trice. I will never forget what almost the first words he said to me were. After examining the size of each of our hands he informed me that, because of smaller hands than the other guys on the crew, I was going to be the #3 man on the crew. I later learned why this was an advantage to

have
smaller
hands.
He told
me that
I would
probably
curse
him for
this

selection because of the job that the #3 man did on various weapons loads. I determined right then and there that, instead of cursing him, I was going to

20

give every effort to becoming the best #3 man on the base. While not intending to boast, I feel that I accomplished this when, after a year and a half, I was selected to be the #3 man on the Loading Standardization Crew.

The first months as a weapons loader were very busy months indeed. Time was spent in the load barn getting certified on a number of different load configurations on the F-4D Phantoms which had recently replaced the F-100's that had been at Hahn. I witnessed the departure of the very last F-100 from Hahn. Many years later, while serving as an Instructor at Lowery AFB, I saw this very same F-100 on a pedestal display there.

In addition to certification training, we were also busy with studying CDC courses so that we could upgrade to 5-level status as soon as possible. These were very tiring days, but we were getting accustomed to a really unique way of life.

Life Outside of Work

Life in this very beautiful place was great. Living in the barracks brought some new challenges as we each had to learn to respect others and their desire sometimes for a little quiet time. Working together to keep the place ready to pass room inspection became a routine. Enjoying time together in card games, listening to music, etc., also proved to be very rewarding. Travel opportunities in this part of the world were like a dream come true to this "non-world traveler." One of my greatest regrets, now that I look back at it, is my not availing myself of much more tours, etc., while there. I traded a tape recorder for a vehicle (a 196? Fiat) while there and travelled quite a bit in the local area. However, I wish I had gone to many more other countries than I did. I actually was able to travel to France, Luxembourg, Holland, etc., but there was clearly much more to see than what I actually saw.

TDY's were part of the work requirements while at Hahn. I went twice to Wheelus AB, Tripoli, Libya during my tour in Germany. That was quite an experience, to say the least! I had my first experience of flying on a C-124. It was while in North Africa that I ate camel burgers.

Another great memory from my time at Hahn was that I was able to play in a band while there.  Several other loaders and

23

I formed the group which had several names over the course of time that we were together. We started out as the "Drifterz." We soon changed the name of the band to "The Purple Orangutan." That didn't last very long, however, and we finally settled on "The Forces of Sound." We played quite frequently at the teen club on base as well as a few clubs in some of the surrounding towns. Probably the most memorable one was a place called "The Pferdistal" (not sure of spelling or town where it was located).

Chow Hall

Many in the military spend a fair amount of time complaining. They grumble about a variety of things, but the one which is usually prominent is food at the chow hall. Since loaders had some unusual work requirements, sometimes we were not able to make it to the chow hall during the hours they were open. As a result, we were on "separate rations", which means that we were paid extra each month for rations. When we were able to go to the chow hall we had to pay for meals there. I always enjoyed eating at the chow hall at Hahn and had no complaints whatsoever. My favorite meal of the day was "midnight chow". This usually started at 10:30 PM for the overnight crews. This was a breakfast meal and was fantastic!

Trip to Hospital

Another memory that I still have from my time at Hahn was a late night trip to the hospital. Several of us had been to the NCO Club for a night of entertainment. A fistfight broke out in the club which rapidly escalated to outside in front of the club. I went out to watch the fight. To better see what was going on I stepped up onto a wall in front so I could see over the crowd that had gathered. After a few minutes of little to no activity in the fight, I stepped down and twisted my ankle. I hobbled back to the barracks and tried to go to bed, but could not sleep because of the pain. I arose and discovered that my ankle was very swollen and turning black and blue up to my knee. I decided that I had better have the docs take a look at it. So, I managed to hobble to the hospital which was fairly close to the barracks.

When I arrived there they examined it and informed me that I had torn some ligaments in my ankle and that I would have been better off with a broken ankle. They gave me some pain medication, crutches, and sent me back to the barracks.

Try to imagine, if possible, a first-time-ever experience of using crutches. This was in and of itself a very real challenge. To make things worse, however, was trying to negotiate and maneuver around in the snow and ice. I can recall several times of crutches and myself going separate ways and me landing flat on my back in the snow.

One beauty of the above described situation, however, was that I could always get some good looking young lady in the recreation center to carry my food tray for me. I guess there was a positive in even this bad situation!

German Girlfriend

Another memory which I have is Brigetta. Brigetta was a young, German girl that I met at a club one night. She and I seemed to "hit it off" pretty well. I remember often walking her home in the snow after we had met at some club for a night of music and dancing. I often reflect on this time and regret that I did not insist on her speaking German when we were together. She spoke better English than I did. Had I responded differently I am sure that I could have learned much more German than the few words I did learn.

Interesting Bomb Load Crew Experience

I recall one very "interesting" bomb download that the load crew that I was assigned to experienced. We were all in the shop awaiting the return of the flight of Phantoms that had taken off an hour or so earlier. After their arrival my crew was dispatched to the flight line to download a bomb that was stuck in the rack. The aircraft had taken off with four Napalm dispensers uploaded. Two were on each inboard pylon. When the pilot tried to drop the bombs on target, the bomb on the outboard side of the pylon was struck when the one on the inboard side was dropped and caught by the wind. It hit the one on the outboard side and caused it to be stuck in the rack. The pilot could, therefore, not drop that last bomb.

The plane taxied to a special place that would be safe for us to download the bomb. When we arrived at the site the fire department was standing by and we assessed the situation. There was Napalm leaking all over the plane, the ground, and it seemed like everywhere. While we downloaded the stuck bomb the fire crew members were literally over our shoulders with their fire hoses – just in case. Of all the loads that I was involved in, both nuclear and conventional, this one was the scariest.

Six - Day War

In 1967, a very serious situation arose in the Middle East. War had broken out with Israel and her enemies in the area. We were put on alert for possible involvement. I remember loading weapons (both conventional and nuclear) on every aircraft on base. We packed suitcases and lived in the shop until the situation eased. It was a very unnerving time for all involved.

Going Home

About half way through my tour at Hahn I returned to my home for a thirty - day leave. When I had departed home in 1966, I had no intention of going home until my tour was done. As it turned out, my younger sister was planning a wedding and requested my presence.

The trip was a very relaxing and rewarding experience. I was amazed at how many things had changed at home. Highways were widened and changed significantly. I even missed the turn to go to my home on one of my first excursions.

The wedding was beautiful and the time at home passed rather quickly. Then it was time to head back to Germany and finish my tour at Hahn. The remaining months there were filled with many of the routine duties that bomb loaders experience as well as some travel and continuance with playing music at various events.

In late summer 1969, I received a set of orders reassigning me to MacDill AFB, Florida. This was sixty days earlier than I was originally scheduled to leave. In August I packed the remaining things that I had not shipped home into my suitcase and travelled back to Frankfurt where it all began and boarded a homebound plane. When I left Germany, a part of me remained. It has been many, many years now since that final day. My military career continued for many more (nearly 38 total) years, but I will always look back at my time at Hahn with fondness and gratitude that I was able to be a part of this wonderful experience for nearly three years. Much more could probably be included here, but I had determined to be somewhat brief. I probably did not do very well in this regard.

If anyone is interested, I have written another book (actually several to be exact) relating to my military life. The book is entitled, <u>A Lifer's Life</u> which includes much of what I have shared here, but much more as well. Contact me at <u>spectrejim@yahoo.com</u> for more information about this book as well as others.

NOW FOR MANY MORE MEMORIES FROM MANY OTHERS WHO HAVE RESPONDED BY E-MAIL, FACEBOOK, OR OTHER MEDIA FORMS.

Abel, David

David went to Hahn in 1973, right after tech school and stayed until 1976. He lived off base while there. David was a 462xx (Weapons Mechanic).

He traveled to Holland, Luxembourg, Belgium, Switzerland, and Spain. He also made a trip home while at Hahn.

David's favorite memory is the wine fest at Cochem. Least favorites include base alerts, ORI's and TDY deployments.

After his tour at Hahn was complete he returned to the States for reassignment.

Abell, Tammy

Tammy was at Hahn from July 1989 until March 1990, coming right after basic training and tech school. She worked in Supply at Metro Tango. Favorite memories are: touring the castles, travel to Trabach and K-town. Her worst memory is her boss, who she describes as, "Such a jerk (an alcoholic jerk).

She did not return home during her stint at Hahn and says that she wishes that she could have stayed longer.

Adams, Doug

Doug's time at Hahn was from August, 1985 until March, 1989. Hahn was Doug's first duty assignment. His AFSC was 55550.

Favorite memories for Doug are, "My landlords Rolf and Tina and their families. They are, to this day, like family to me. I went back over there in November, 2013 and stayed with them for two weeks. First time seeing them in 25 years and it was like I never left.

I also had great AF people that I worked with. I spent about a year and 8 months at Wuscheim AS at 50th CES Det-1 and loved every minute of it.

His worst memory is, "Getting forgotten and left for 18 hours in 40 degree weather while playing SP augmentee during a NATO Tac Eval. (That would surely be a bad memory!!)

Alexander, Barbara

I am interested!! I'd like to share about the mud fights we had behind the barracks. A group of us medics were covered in mud, laughing and blowing off steam when the klaxon sounded. No time to shower...just showed up at the hospital in chem gear with mud undergarments. (I'm not sure we were even drinking that day.)

Anonymous

One who wishes to remain anonymous reports that he was stationed at Hahn from January 1987 until 1991. It was his second tour of duty after tech school. He returned to the States while at Hahn for a funeral and a divorce.

His AFSC was 431X1B (Crew chief). He lived on base for part of his time at Hahn. He also lived in Heinzerath and then Soren.

Most favorite memories include winefests, and traveling to Holland and Israel. Least favorite memory is the long hours in a gas mask.

After leaving Hahn he returned to the States and was reassigned to a "special duty" assignment.

Anonymous

Another anonymous responder states that he was at Hahn from 87 – 90 after serving at a previous location.

He was married when he arrived and worked as a 57170.

His most favorite memory was the wine-fests. His worst memory was arriving at Hahn with no sponsor.

After completion of his tour at Hahn he was reassigned to another stateside base. He rates his experience at Hahn as "enjoyable."

Beck, Charlene

Charlene arrived at Hahn on 12/3/1979 and stayed until 9/3/1983.It was not a first assignment for her. While at Hahn she lived off base, fist at Unzenberg and then Kirchberg-Denzen.

Her duty assignment was as a USAF Nurse (9756?). While at Hahn she returned to the States twice on emergency leave due to illness in the family and for a death in the family.

Charlene shares her favorite memories as boat rides on the Mosel, dinner out at great German Gausthauses, shopping, and ballet in Trier. Her least favorite memories were stated as midnight to noon war games shifts and ambulance rides to accompany bodies to Weisbaden.

At the end of her tour at Hahn she was assigned to Shaw AFB, SC.

Her son was born at Hahn in 1981. She refers to her years at Hahn as, "the happiest years of my life."

Bennett, William

William served at Hahn from 1961 – 1964. It was his first assignment after basic, etc. He served as a firefighter (57130).

William lived on base for his tour at Hahn.

As for best memories he says, "I don't really have a favorite. All are good memories. William did not return home during his years at Hahn.

After leaving Hahn he returned to Florida.

Blankenship, James

James was at Hahn from 1984 – 1987 after having served at a previous assignment. He was single when he arrived at Hahn and was a 46252.

While at Hahn, James traveled to

England and also returned to the States to get married.

His most favorite memory is that he met his wife and that both children were born at Hahn.

After leaving Hahn he returned to the States for reassignment. He describes his years at Hahn as, "the best."

Branks, David S.

David went to Hahn in March 1973 and departed in January, 1977 after having been at MacDill AFB training for Viet Nam. He was married while at Hahn.

David was a J43151C and enjoyed at least one trip to Holland while at Hahn. He also was able to return home while stationed there.

His most favorite memories include: "the people, our son's birth, lasting friendships, holidays, and working with many professionals."

His worst memory is the driving restrictions because of the energy crisis in the States.

After leaving Hahn he returned to the States for reassignment. He rates his time at Hahn as, "the best."

He concluded his remarks with this statement (one that many of us share!): "The saddest thing is not being able to go back in time and serve in the Air Force again!"

Brown, Dave

Dave went to Hahn from March, 1984 till Sept, 1989 for his second tour of duty. While at Hahn he lived both on base and off base in Zell, Buch, Traben-Trarbach and Kinheim. Dave's AFSC was 2a0x1b.

Dave was able to travel to France, Luxembourg, Italy, and Austria during his tour at Hahn.

He lists his favorite memories as, "Winefests...met my wife there (1986)....and softball (lots of softball)." Unpleasant memory stated by Dave is LSNs.

Dave made a trip back to the States during his time at Hahn and upon completion of the tour he returned to the States for reassignment.

Burhans, Bill

Bill was a 431x1 and was stationed at Hahn from May, 1978 until May, 1980. It was his first duty assignment after basic and school.

Bill was single at Hahn and lived off base.

His best memories include playing

soccer on the base team while his worst is the 5 day Salty Nation exercises.

Bill returned to the States during his stay at Hahn and states that his family was stationed in Berlin, Germany during his assignment.

He says that his time at Hahn was "enjoyable". At the end of his tour he was reassigned to a stateside base.

Capella, Karen

Karen was at Hahn from 1988 until 1991and says that it was her first duty assignment. She was a dependent wife and worked at the N.C.O. club. Winefests are her favorite memory from Hahn. She did return home at some time during her time at Hahn.

Chabot, Chris

Chris was at Hahn from 89 - 93. During this time he was a teen-age dependent. He stated that he did work with the MP's during the summer months.

Chris's favorite memories from time at Hahn are "being a teenager and having the best times of my life with awesome people and friends."

His most unpleasant experience included "getting in trouble with the MP's and Polizei for something my friend and I didn't do. Those Polizei don't (bleep) around at all let me tell you. Machine guns drawn in our faces right away."

Chris says that he did not return to home during his stay at Hahn.

In reference to additional information he wished to share on the survey he says, "I was a dependent so I can't answer all of the questions, but my time there was just the most amazing time of my life. Got to work with the MP's, got to hang out in the 496ᵗʰ hangars with the F-16's from time to time since my dad had very good connections. Met some of the coolest people that I still stay in contact with."

Chancellor, William R.

William was an Air Policeman who was stationed at Hahn from 1958 - 1962. He went to Hahn after serving at a previous assignment. While at Hahn, William lived on base for three years and off base for the last year.

Travel opportunities for William included France, Holland, Luxembourg, and Italy.

His most favorite memories are being able to see so many historic places and meeting many wonderful friends. Worst memory is the continual alerts.

After Hahn, William returned to the States for reassignment.

He further states that he returned to Germany about seven years ago and was able to visit the Hahn area and it brought back so many memories.

Clatterbuck, Ricky

Ricky served at Hahn from 1979 until 1981. This was his first assignment after basic and school. His career field was in the Security Police area. Travel, friends, and parties are his fondest memories from this time. His worst memory is, "weird weather."

Ricky returned home once during his stay at Hahn due to a death in the family. He says that it was the best assignment he had.

Clinesmith, Matthew

I was born there in 87. I would definitely read a book if one is available.

Collard, Marlene

Marlene was at Hahn from September, 1977 until May 1984. She had previously spent six months stateside then did a joint spouse tour at Hahn. She went to Hahn as Marlene Satchell, then divorced and married D Griffin.

Marlene worked as a 67270 - Accounting and Finance troop.

While at Hahn she traveled to France.

Her most favorite memory is everyone looking out for everyone else because no family was around. Worst memory is full chem. gear in the middle of a hot summer.

While at Hahn Marlene returned home when her sister lost her baby to SIDS and also returned for a divorce.

After Hahn she returned for a stateside assignment. She rates her time at Hahn as "the best" and says that she would love to return for a visit.

Marlene also shares that she lived on the economy for many years and then lived in base housing. She was there during the Baader Meinhoff era, bombing in K-town, locals asking her to purchase for them, contract housing. She was in charge of government property lost, stolen, or destroyed and reports it as a "big farce." She saw contracts for painting houses, then replace windows and "screw up paint." She also says that she saw much female discrimination while there.

Coviello, Daniel

Daniel was stationed at Hahn during the time period of 85 - 87. His earlier assignment had been at Minot AFB, ND. I guess the cold and snow, etc. was nothing new when he arrived at Hahn.

His AFSC is reported to have been 81150.

Daniel says that his most favorite memories from Hahn revolve around being involved in German Hunting. He also was involved with a Bugle Group in Kastellaun which was used for signaling hunting. He also fondly remembers the lifelong friends he made.

Daniel states that he did not take leave and return home during his time at Hahn.

Crouch, Randy

Randy was stationed at Hahn from Aug 89 until May 93 and states that it was not his first duty station. He lived in Lautsenhausen for a year and then moved on base.

Randy had the privilege of traveling to Belgium, Luxembourg, France, and the Netherlands while at Hahn.

His AFSC was 1C370.

Randy's best memories are travelling, castles, food, fests, and friends. His worst memories are winters, exercises, and the bowling alley fire.

After his tour at Hahn was complete he returned to the States for reassignment. He did not return home during his stay at Hahn but states that his wife did.

Cyrus

Cyrus was at HAFB from 8/88 – 4/91. This was his first duty assignment. Cyrus worked as a Security specialist.

Cyrus states that he, also, was able to return home during his stay at Hahn.

After his assignment he returned to the States for reassignment.

Cyrus lived on base during his time there and rates it as, "the best."

Dittmar, Jeanette

Jeanette was at Hahn from 1973 through 1975. Her favorite memory is "hanging out in the woods next to base housing." Least favorite memory was, "waking up to base alert." She did not return home during her time at Hahn.

Jeanette commented. "I loved my time at Hahn. I would not replace it for anything." (I certainly would concur with her final statement.)

Doutt, Don

Don was at Hahn from Mar 1961 – Apr 1964. His assignment was in the 50th Combat Support Group, 50th TFW, where he worked in Statistical Services (data processing).

Don's favorite memory was travelling to other parts of Europe. He stated that his most disliked memory involved standing alerts in the cold and snow.

Don is another who did not return home during his time at Hahn.

Don lived at Hahn for 1 ½ years before he got married in the base chapel to a girl from home (NC). After getting married he and his new wife lived in Sohren until returning to the States.

Duval, Mary

Mary was at Hahn from December 1978 - November 1981. Her husband had been stationed at Hurlburt Field, Florida prior to their arrival at Hahn. (I spent some time in the Hurlburt Fiels area as well. Another great assignment!) She returned home once, in September, 1979.

While stationed at Hahn Mary says that she got to travel to the Netherlands, Spain, France, Belgium, Austria, and Switzerland. They lived in Kirschburg and Sohren.

Mary's husband was a Security Policeman while at Hahn. She says that she and her husband served together.

Favorite memories from their time at Hahn include, "Playing softball and volleyball on the base teams, visiting other countries, being a part of Hahn Baptist church and having their daughter at Hahn in 1981. She says that she does not hav any bad memories.

After completion of their time at Hahn they returned to the states for discharge.

Ethier, Omer

Omer was assigned to Hahn from 76 – 79. He states that this was not his first duty assignment.

His AFSC was 43171C.

Omer's favorite memories from Hahn were "the people and the sights." I think this would probably be a favorite among many of us. I know for sure that it is with me.

Omer's least favorite remembrances were the long hours, and lots of TDY's.

Omer said that he did return home, at least once, while he was stationed at Hahn.

He said that he had a total of 26 years of service and that Hahn was the closest bunch of people for him and his family.

Ethier, Sally

We were stationed at Hahn AFB from 1978 to 1981. Loved the area. Left there to go to Kaiserslautern for the I G team.

Falack, Larry

"I was stationed at Hahn Air Base from October 1966 through November 1969. I was assigned to the 496th FIS as an aircraft armament specialist, loading missiles and rockets on the F-102 Delta Daggers. I was single then, and lived in the barracks across from the chapel. It was far from luxurious, with six to eight men per room, so we tended not to spend much time in the barracks.

Due to the lack of available women, and the abundance of places to drink, i.e., Airman's Club, NCO Club, Rod and Gun Club, Bowling Alley, and the bars on the economy, we spent most of our nights getting inebriated. Occasionally, one of us would buy a car and we would chase the women in Traben-Trarbach, Bernkastel-Kues, and other small towns. Unfortunately, that usually led to trouble, so we tended to stay on base.

We often had shop parties with all the officers, NCO's, airmen and their families. We had wonderful times and became very close. As a single man, I was invited to many of their homes. I would love to be able to get in touch with anyone that was stationed there with me.

Things I remember about Hahn Air Base, not necessarily in order of importance.

• The inter-base football games, especially the homecoming games and parades.

• The beer tent outside the NCO Club over the summer holidays.

• Stag night at the NCO Club.

• The First G (First Gasthaus outside

the   gate).

• Hiding upstairs at the First G, until the Air Police and German police inspected at closing time, and then drinking at the back bar until daylight.

• The Farmer's Breakfast at the First G.

• Ordering a bottle of Cognac, a bottle of Coke and a bowl of ice to celebrate New Year's Eve at the First G.

• Going to Ushi's Bratwurst Stand in Lautzenhausen for bratwurst, hahnchen, schnitzel or schaschlik.

• The wine fests at Zell, Bernkastel and many other Mosel River towns.

• The steaks at the Rod and Gun Club.

• The Airman's Club, NCO Club and the bands of the month, especially the Zara's.

• The waitress at the Airman's Club, Anna, with whom I fell in love.

• Going to the base theater and standing for the National Anthem.

• Fasching and the Wittlich Swinefest.

- Parkbrau   Beer.
- Jagermeister, Ratzenputz and playing dice   with   beer   coasters.
- TDY   to   Munich   and   Madrid.
- The fog. I may be exaggerating, but I believe that one year we only saw the sun 21 days.

Filipiak, Joe

Joe's service at Hahn began in October 1981 and ended in October 1985. He had been assigned elsewhere previously.
His AFSC was 81170.

Favorite memories for Joe are: "The Mosel River area, Trauben Traubach and other great river towns. Although the circumstances were not good, I will always treasure the two times I was in charge of Security Forces deployed to F-16 crash sites. Will always remember the exceptional bunch of guys who worked their butts off in harsh, trying conditions." Worst memories are: "TAC

Evals, Nuclear Security Inspections (NSI), ORI.

Fleming, Mike

Mike served at Hahn from April 1965 to April 1967. Hahn was not his first duty assignment.

Mike lived on base for a while in Dorm 313. After this he moved to Peterswald and Morbach.

Mike was a 29150 while at Hahn.

His most favorite memories are: the people, ie Germans off base and the Air force troops he served with. He also owned a Quarter Midget race car powered be 250 CC motorcycle engine. They also had their own oval race track. In addition, he raced at Rhein Main, Sembach, and Ramstein.

He says that the weather is his worst memory. He loved the snow (he was from the South) but hated the ice.

After leaving Hahn Mike was

reassigned to tnhe Aeronautical map and Information Center, 2nd and Arsenal Streets, St. Louis, MO.

He is returning to the area in September of 2015. He says that he iw sure he will be disappointed but can't wait to see what is left of the old base.

Gaffney, TSgt Joseph T.

Joseph was stationed at Hahn from Nov 3rd until Apr 9th, 1993 after having served at another assignment. He lived off base in Lotzbeuren and base housing.

His AFSC at Hahn was 304x4, 2E1x3 – Ground Radio Communications Specialist in the 2184th Communications Squadron.

While at Hahn he was able to travel to Austria, Italy, France, Luxembourg, Belgium, and the Netherlands.

Most favorite memories include living in the local community, getting to know local customs, and experiencing the culture. Least favorite were the exercises and chem gear.

Joseph was at Hahn at the time of closure. A reassignment team came to Hahn and he chose to stay in USAFE at RAF Mildenhall, England.

Gal, Michael

Michael was at Hahn from Apr 1986 - Aug 1991. That was a lengthy tour during which time he, undoubtedly, saw and experienced much. This was not his first assignment either.

Michael's AFSC was 42672. This identifies a Jet Engine Technician.

Michael also returned home at least once during his tour at Hahn.

Gantz, Denny

Denny was assigned to Hahn from 7/81-1/86, after having served elsewhere. He lived off base in Bishofsdhrone, near Morbac. He was a jet engine mechanic (C42670).

Denny loved travelling while at Hahn and says that he traveled to "too many places to list." He did return home while there. His worst memory is, like many others, the chem. games.

Denny retired at Hahn and became a dependent spouse. He refers to his time at Hahn as the "best assignment ever."

Givens, Tom & Peggy

The Givens were at Hahn from August 1984 to July 1991. It was not a first duty assignment for them. While at Hahn they lived in Lower Kirchberg housing area.

Job duty at Hahn was as a Physician Assistance.

Most favorite memory is how everyone got along like we were a team. Worst memory was the bombings.

After leaving Hahn they returned to the States for reassignment.

Closing comments from the Givens: " Loved Hahn. Everyone was like a family and we depended on each other when there was a need. Excited for others during special occasions. One of the best bases we were ever at. Made many good friends and endless memories. Thank you Hahn."

GN

This person served at Hahn from Nov 85 – Nov 87 and lived off base. He/she came to Hahn for a first assignment after a 22 month long tech school. AFSC is list4ed as 20833C.
He/she worked at 6911th ESS at Metro Tango.

Travel opportunities while at Hahn include France, Austria, Switzerland, Holland, Luxembourg, Belgium,

Liechtenstein, Spain, Italy, Greece.

Most favorite memories include "Attending the Bizzarefest concerts at Lorelei on the Rhein."

After completing the tour at Hahn they did an in-theatre transfer to support 691st ESW Detachment 4 at Stuttgart Army airfield and then stayed an additional year as a contractor for VII Corps.

Gobel, William

William was a dependent who was at Hahn from 1963 - 1967. He lived in Simmern and Buchen Bueren.

His most favorite memory is:" **Christmas eve .... '65 ...** channel 22 breaks in and announces a RADAR contact north and that jets have been scrambled to intercept. Outside you can hear the phantoms taking off and, yes, those were some LOUD SOBs. We were scared for the first time and I was only 12. Two hours later, they break in again with a live audio feed from the lead phantom and he describes the bogey as a reindeer team pulling a large red sleigh, fat man piloting the rig. Says the pilot waved to them and they returned the wave."

William says that his worst memory is going to school there.

After leaving Hahn, he wound up at Westover, MA, then Homestead, FL, and finally at Lackland, TX.

Grace, Jack

Jack came to Hahn in 1981 and stayed until 1986. He came straight to Hahn after basic training and tech school. His AFSC was 423x5. He lived off base while at Hahn.

Travel is the best memory Jack has from his time at Hahn. He traveled to Holland, Belgium, France, Luxembourg, Spain, Andorra, Denmark, England,

Ireland, Switzerland, Liechtenstein, East Germany (DDR). Jack did return home while stationed at Hahn.

His worst memories are listed as two individuals - MSgt Bob Stolt and Lt Col Jessie Helms.

When the end of his tour at Hahn arrived he did a continuous tour to Soestererg AB, NL.

Grider, Thomas

Thomas was stationed at Hahn form Feb. 1984 - Sep. 1991. Hahn was not his first duty assignment.

Thomas' AFSC was 423X1.

He travelled to Spain while at Hahn.

His most favorite memory from his time there was meeting and marrying his wife.

The memory that he remembers as

least favorite was the weather.

Thomas stated that he returned home from Hahn while assigned there.

He concluded his entry on the survey by stating that his time at Hahn was, "The time of my life."

Gwen

Gwen arrived, for her first assignment, at Hahn in 1981 and stayed until 1985. She lived in the dorm until she had a baby and got married. She then moved to Sohren.

Gwen's AFSC at Hahn was 425x3.

She says that she didn't want to be at Hahn, at first, because of feeling alone and lost. She did, however, enjoy taking road trips to the river or just around the countryside.

At the end of her tour at Hahn Gwen was reassigned to Luke AFB, Arizona.

Hahaj, John

John arrived at Hahn in Feb 1961 for his first duty assignment and stayed until Feb 64. He was a 77150 and lived on base while at Hahn.

John was able to travel to Holland, France, and Luxemburg during his stay in Europe. He did not return home during this time.

His most favorite memory centers on spending Christmas in Paris. His least favorite memory is ORIs.

After his time at Hahn was complete he returned to the States for reassignment.

Hall, Charles David

I was at Hahn from 11Feb1971 to 10Mar 197(?). Played on the base baseball team and base football team -

#43, LB. Didn't want to leave.

Hamm, Steven

Steven served at Hahn as a 43151C. He was at Hahn from June 5, 1974 through June 5, 1976.

At the top of the list of favorite things to do for Steven is "wine fests." (He shares this pastime with many who have written.)

Least favorite remembrances from his time at Hahn include, "Cloudy all the time during winter months. Was dreary!"

Harr, John

John was stationed at Hahn from January 1975 until Jan 1981 and says that it was not his first assignment. He did not return home during his stay at Hahn. His AFSC was 54270. John's favorite memories from Hahn were camping on the Mosel River each summer in a town called Wolf. He also enjoyed drinking beer. Wearing the chem gear during exercises was his least favorite memory.

Harrell, Todd

Todd was at Hahn from April 84 to April 86. It was his first duty assignment after tech school. He was an airframe repair specialist and lived in the dorms.

Todd's favorite memory was the wind fests and his worst is the war games.

While at Hahn, Todd traveled to Turkey, Spain, Sweden, Switzerland, Austria, and Holland.

Upon leaving Hahn John was reassigned to Holloman AFB.

Harthorn, Casey

After a previous assignment Casey went to Hahn in 1984. He stayed until 1991. His AFSC at Hahn was T42390. He lived off base at Gonzerath.

While at Hahn Casey traveled to Turkey Spain, and Israel. He also did return home during his tour at Hahn.

Casey says that his favorite memory is the Volksmarch with family and friends. His worst memory is "alarm red."

When his tour was complete at Hahn he returned to the States for reassignment to Cannon AFB, New Mexico.

Haskell, Larry

Larry was at Hahn from June, 1972 through July, 1974 as his first duty assignment. He lived on base while at Hahn, in barracks #302. His AFSC was 81150.

While at Hahn, Larry says that his best memories are "F-4's!!!! Watching, hearing, feeling that awesome airplane! Camaraderie in the Squadron; food and beer; great German people!"

His worst memories are Many, many alerts; weather at times.

After leaving Hahn he returned to Minot AFB, ND. He says that Hahn was the best assignment he had in all of his 20+ years. He did go on to fly – driven by the dream that took root at Hahn.

Haverty, Terry

Terry's time to Hahn was from March, 1985 to May 1989. This was not her first assignment. Her ex-husband came to Hahn after two previous assignments. They lived both on and off base.

Terry's ex-husband was an Ammo troop. (I was one of those also. In fact, that was my final AFSC at retirement time.)

As for favorite memories, she says that she loved "all of it". Her brother was stationed at Bitburg at the same time they were at Hahn. Her middle daughter was born at Hahn in '87. She states that it was her second time living in Germany since she is an "Army BRAT".

Terry's worst memory is that her ex-husband never went TDY and that they never went anywhere. She never returned home during her stay at Hahn.

After leaving Hahn they were reassigned to Norton AFB, California. Her concluding remark was that it was an "awesome assignment!!!!!!" (I think that many of us would certainly agree with Terry on this final remark.)

Hensley, Glen

Glen was stationed at Hahn from 3/79 - 3/81 after having served at a previous assignment. His AFSC was 81150 and he lived off base in Sohren.

In June, 1980 Glen took a month of leave and returned home for a visit.

While at Hahn Glen traveled to Belgium, Luxembourg, Holland, and went TDY to Norway.

Favorite memories include, "Frauleins, food, scenery, wine/beer, culture." Least favorite memory is the alerts.

Glen says that Germany was awesome and that he would have had even more fun but "the Air Force kept getting in the way."

After Hahn Glen returned to the States for discharge.

Hilbrandt, Brian

Brian went to Hahn as his first duty assignment in Jan, 81 and stayed until Jan, 83. He was a 431x1 and lived in Lautzenhausen.

He traveled during his stay at Hahn to Spain and France. He also made a trip home during his tour.

His favorite memories are the people, food, wine festivals and traveling around the country.

He returned to the States after his time at Hahn for reassignment.

Hinshaw(Boudreau), Colleen

Colleen was a crew chief that arrived at Hahn in June 1985 and stayed until Aug 1986. It was her first assignment after tech school. She lived on base during her stay at Hahn.

While there she traveled to Turkey, Spain, Austria, France, and England.

Her most favorite memories include, "the people, the beauty of the country, winefests, and my best is meeting my husband to be!" Colleen mentions as her worst memories, "weather and commanding officers."

After completion of the tour at Hahn Colleen returned home for discharge. She says that she misses the people she met there. For her it was a once in a lifetime experience that she would repeat "in a hot second!"

Hockley, Karen

"I have been thinking about what to write and this evening Jennifer reminded me of our (Rod's and mine) recreation while we were at Hahn Air Base. Our weekend 'recreation, 'in our apartment after we bought our 1969 VW Beetle, was to take our VW to the shop to wash it once a week, and to wax it every other weekend. Rod wanted to make sure the salt from the roads was washed away. The second time Rod went to Libya on TDY I decided I needed to buy groceries so I went to the BX. When I had completed my shopping I took my groceries out to our VW and found I had locked my keys in the car. The consequence of my trip to purchase groceries was that our landlord in Sohren had to have the door to our apartment taken off so I could get my extra set of keys. I slept in our apartment for the next two nights without a door. Fortunately the door was inside the landlord's house."

(Note: Karen is Rod Hockley's wife and Jennifer is their daughter. Rod was a former roommate of mine and also a fellow member of the band that we played together in. Sadly, Rod passed away a few years ago after a lengthy illness.)

Hugli, Dennis L.

Dennis worked as a Nav Sys specialist (T32871) while at Hahn. His favorite memory is the German friends they made during the 8 ½ years they were at Hahn.He says his worst memory is the dumping of the honey wagons. (Yeah, I remember that also!) He says that, "Rhaund was the best to live in."

Huie, Allen

Allen was at HAFB from 7 Dec 1988 till 16 Oct 1991. His first duty assignment prior to Hahn was at Dobbins AFB.

Allen's AFSC was 42652.

His favorite memories include, "The people, as our son had adoptive Grand Parents while there – Fray Muller and her boyfriend Ludwig who were both in their 70's. They made holidays special like putting up the Easter egg tree". He also says that "Team work during Desert Shield/Storm" is a good memory.

Allen's least favorite was, like others, "Exercises."

Allen stated that he returned home on emergency leave while at Hahn for his brother's funeral.

He concluded the survey by stating, "I wish my 23 year Air Force career could have all been at Hahn AB." He misses his German friends.

Hunter   (Deering),
Stacey

Stacey's dates of assignment at Hahn are April, 1982 - 1985. She came to Hahn right after tech school.

Stacy lived in the female barracks at first. She later got married and rented a house in Loffelscheid.

Her AFSC at Hahn was 29170.

Most favorite memories include: weinfests!! Shooting darts at the nco club, seeing Europe!! Love, love, loved all the traveling I was able to do! Seeing historical places vs reading about them!!! There was nothing that she saw as unfavorable.

Stacey returned to the States twice during her years at Hahn. Once to get married and once two years later.

After her tour was complete she returned to the States for discharge.

Hylton, John

John served at Hahn from Dec 1981 – Dec 1983. He had previously been at Incirlik CDI, Turkey.

John was single at Hahn and served as a 64570. He lived off base while at Hahn. He stayed at Hahn his entire tour without making a trip home. He did make a trip to Luxembourg.

His most favorite memories are: "The volksmarches, touring down on the Mosel River, visiting in Bavaria – the Eagles Nest and local area."

His least favorite moments at Hahn were the Salty Nations exercises – NATO-TAC EVAL.

He rated his time at Hahn as enjoyable and says that he would love to return for a visit. He says that he probably worked harder and longer hours than anywhere before or after Hahn due to going through the F-4 to F-16 conversion, but it was one of the most gratifying assignments.

After leaving Hahn he returned to the States for reassignment.

Ickes, Eugene M.

Eugene arrived at Hahn in 1980 and departed in 1983. It was not his first duty assignment. His AFSC was in the Postal field (99604). Team work is listed as Eugene's best memory from his time at Hahn. He lists as his worst – "Too many war games." He follows this up by stating, "…but it was necessary." He did not return home until his tour was complete at Hahn.

Ipock, Linn

I was there 85 - 87. During my time, Chernobyl had a meltdown, mad cow disease, and Hahn was giving away 10 lbs (I think) of American beef, steaks, ground beef, etc. Cooked many ribs behind gold section tool crib... right beside triple deuce (Bldg. 222).

Linn states that Hahn was his second duty station and that he lived off base in Oberklienich and Peterswald. While at Hahn he traveled to Luxembourg, Belgium, and France.

Linn, like myself, was a weapons troop (46250) at Hahn. He, like many others, liked the winefests and disliked 12 - 14 hour shifts and exercises.

After completion of his tour he returned stateside for reassignment. He did make a trip home during his tour and says that his time at Hahn was a "GREAT ASSIGNMENT"

Jim

Jim was stationed at Hahn from May, 1988 to May, 1991. He went to Hahn after a previous assignment.

Jim was a 462 (Weapons Specialist) who lived on base for the first 9 months. He then moved to Biebern for the rest of his time at Hahn.

Jim went TDY to Turkey and Spain. His leisure travel included trips to France, Belgium, Holland, and Austria. He also made a trip back to the U S in August, 1990. When he arrived at DFW he found out about the mess that wa kicking up in Kuwait.

His best memories are the travelling opportunities he had while at Hahn. Worst memory is the entire "BS" he had to put up with on base and in the work center.

Overall, "the time spent at Hahn was a good one. Have made some lifelong friendships."

Johnson, Carla Tucker

I was a DoDDS teacher a short time and Schools Liaison and Dependent Misconduct Officer, 89-92 for Base Commander. I have good memory so would be happy to answer questions you might have.

Kellner, Steven

Steven was at Hahn from 8/1985 until 3/1988. He came to Hahn from another previous assignment. His AFSC was 20150.

His most favorite memories from Hahn include having a great job, good friends, and living on the Mosel River. He says that the snow is his worst memory.

King, Ricky

Ricky's dates of assignment to Hahn are from July 1987 through July 1990. Hahn was not his first duty assignment. Ricky was a 423x0 (rivet force worker). He declares his favorite memories as "Friends, Wine Fests, and Hahn Hawk football games." Least favorite memories – "Chem gear exercises (way too many of those)". Ricky stayed at Hahn until his tour was complete and did not return home during this time. He states further, "We were able to visit many more countries than I was able to check (on the survey). We had a great time at Hahn and brought home a lifetime worth of memories."

Kiser, Chris

Chris lived at Hahn, as a dependent child, from January 1973 until May 1976. Most favorite memories include "Mosel river cruises, annual bazzar, Boy Scouts, Volksmarches, San Remo Pizza, Trier, friends." He says his least favorite memories are, "Watching friends transfer/leave and lose touch with them in a pre-Internet/Facebook era." Chris is another, of many, who did not return to his home at any time during his stay at Hahn. Among countries visited during his stay at Hahn he lists England, Spain, France, Holland, Austria, Belgium, Switzerland. His favorite was Luxembourg.

Kosmicki, Dale

Dale was stationed at Hahn from May 1972 until June 1973. This was his first duty assignment after basic and tech school. Dale's AFSC was 81130 which was Security Police. Dale states that favorite memories include "Growing up!" He also enjoyed going to work every day because, as he says, "We were one big family." His least favorite memory was the last day of Midnight Shift. Losing a day to sleep meant one day less to enjoy Europe.

Dale says that he returned home for Thanksgiving, but that he "Should have stayed in Germany."

Additional information regarding his time at Hahn is summarized as follows:

"I'm currently 62 years old. When I turned 60 someone asked me what my best year ever was. It was that one year I spent at Hahn. It seems like everything I saw or did there had an impact on the rest of my life. I am struck by the fact that I have a lifetime worth of memories packed into One year."

Knowlton, Gary

I was stationed at Hahn AB from March 1965 until February 1968. I was attached to the 50th Air Police Squadron. I took all of my leaves to travel extensively throughout Europe, visiting LONDON, PARIS, ROME, SWITZERLAND, DENMARK, SWEDEN, HOLLAND, AUSTRIA, and LUXEMBOURG. I never returned home until my tour was over. I really was not a fan of the base itself; I loved being and traveling in EUROPE. I attained the rank of SERGEANT, and upon returning home for 30 days I then was assigned to Ellsworth AFB in Rapid City SD for 6 months and was then honorably discharged.

Gary Knowlton , Wheeling, WV

Krage, John

John served at Hahn from Dec 86 until Dec 88. It was a first assignment after tech school for him. A Day trip to other countries is his fondest memory. John also stayed at Hahn until his tour was complete.

John worked in Inventory Management while at Hahn.

He lived off base while at Hahn in the town of Altlay.

While at Hahn he travelled to Turkey, Spain, Belgium and Luxemburg.

John says that he did not appreciate his time while there but he does in hindsight. He further says that he did not (like so many others) like the chemical warfare exercises.

After his tour at Hahn was finished, he returned to the states for reassignment at Mountain Home AFB, Idaho. (I spent some time there as well, though not in a military status.)

Lamp, Michael

Michael went to Hahn in June, 1974, right after tech school and stayed until July 4, 1976. He was a F-4D crew chief (43171C) and lived on base.

While at Hahn, Michael traveled to England, France, Spain, and Belgium. He also returned home twice.

His most favorite memories are: "Many rock concerts, wine-fests, and hiking the countryside. Least favorites are: "The initial culture shock and TAC Evals.

After completion of his tour at Hah, Michael returned to the States where he was assigned to Hill AFB, Ogden, Utah.

He says that he was always looking forward to getting "back to the world" until he realized how much he missed the people, the country, and his job there.

Lane, Shannon

Shannon served at Hahn from Oct 89 - Oct 91. It was her first duty assignment as a POL troop (63501).

Shannon lived off base in the city of Hahn, Fronhoffen, and Ronden.

While at Hahn she traveled to the Netherlands. She did not return home during her tour at Hahn.

Shannon's favorite memories include driving around and visiting the castle ruins. Her least favorite is "Work after all the F-16's moved to other locations. Finding work for 60 plus POL people to perform and management just looking to write people up for anything.

After her time at Hahn Shannon returned to the States for reassignment.

Laskaris, Chris

Chris' assignment at Hahn was from 1979 until 1982.It was not his first duty assignment. His AFSC was 43171c.

His fondest memory is "Drinking at the Dolly Bar." His worst memory is the exercises.

Lastort, Mike

Mike arrived at Hahn in January 1984 and stayed until January 1987. He came to Hahn right after tech school. He worked as a computer operator at Hahn. He says that the AFSC was 511x1 (he thinks). It later changed to 491x1.

Mike's favorite memory is "Living in Traben-Trarbach." NATO exercises are his worst memory.

Mike visited many other countries during his time at Hahn including Luxembourg, France, Belgium, Netherlands, Austria.

Lee

Lee spent the years 78 – 80 at Hahn and says that it was his first duty assignment. Lee was a "462" (Weapons specialist – one that he and I share) while at Hahn.

Concerning his most favorite memories Lee states "Living in Traben. Weekends in the park on the river. Visiting with friends and strangers who passed by. One day a group of tourists got off the bus and we're walking along BIOS watching us throw a Frisbee. One of the gentlemen on the bus heard us speaking English. He said, 'Are you from the United States?' We said, 'Yes, we live here.' He said, 'I cannot believe this. I have earned money and worked."

Ley, Steve

Steve was at Hahn from 1984 to 1987

after having served at another location. While there he lived off base. He rented the main floor of a German family home in Beltheim. His AFSC at Hahn was 423x3.

Steve's best memories at Hahn were the festivals along the Mosel River and the castle tours. His worst memory is the weather.

After leaving Hahn, Steve returned to the States for discharge. However, before the end of terminal leave he flew back to Hahn and re-enlisted.

Lobus, Mike

Mike went to Hahn from Tech School in March, 86 and stayed until April, 89. He worked in the Liquid Fuels Shop (54551). Mike lived off base while at Hahn.

His most favorite memory is living off base and seeing the country. He says that his worst memory is, "rain, rain, rain, and Chem Gear."

97

After leaving Hahn, Mike returned to the States for reassignment to Bergstrom AFB, Texas. He states (like many of the rest of us) that he would love to revisit.

Malcolm, David

David was stationed at Hahn from December, 1985 until April, 1991. He served at a prior assignment before going to Hahn.

David was in the Electro-Environmental career field and lived off base in Kastelon and Bueshenberen. He was the Head Coach of the USAFE Champions Hahn Hawks (89-90). {Congratulations Coach!!!}

His least favorite memory while at Hahn is the weather and Black Ice.

He says that his time at Hahn turned out to be a blessing and a great experience.

After leaving Hahn, David was reassigned to Davis - Monthan AFB, AZ.

McCray (Miller), Deborah A.

Deborah was at Hahn from Feb, 1984 - June, 1987. It was her first duty assignment and she was at Metro Tango. She lived off base, in Morsdorf and Lautzenhausen.

Deborah was a communications specialist (291xx). She travelled to England while stationed at Hahn.

Her best memory is the camaraderie. They did everything in packs - bowling, the club, attending sports events, wine fess, etc.

McGee, Doral

Doral arrived at Hahn in Oct 1969 and stayed until 1973 (the first time). His second tour began in 1980 and lasted until 1984. This was not his

first tour after tech school. Doral had
several AFSCs while at Hahn –
4344(?),43191, and 43171C.

While at Hahn he lived near
Blakenrath in 69 and 70. In 70 – 73 he
was in base housing. In 80 – 84 he
lived in Build Lease Housing in
Rhaunen.

Doral traveled to Italy,
Spain, France, Austria, Netherlands,
Belgium, England, Luxembourg,
Liechenstein.

Favorite memories for Doral
include "The beautiful countryside,
friendly nationals, the new high school
for dependent children, travelling with
the high school teams, volunteering
where needed, Volksmarches, the
friendly town where we lived in build-
lease housing. Also mentioned was
friendships developed with the German
nationals working in the 50th FMS in 69
– 73; traveling all over the Alps with
his wife in a VW bus in the early 70's;
Camping in an Olive orchard in

Florence, near a beach in Malaga, Spain.

Least favorite memories include, "Driving in thick fog with your door open to be able to see the road centerline; wearing the chemical warfare gear."

In the fall of 1973 he returned to the States for reassignment to Fairchild AFB. In the fall of 1984 Doral returned to the States for retirement.

He comments further about the children and their schooling experience by saying, "My older two children attended a few years at Hahn High School; the sports conference for Hahn include Bad K-Army, Bonn, Amsterdam, and two schools in Brussels. The host school team players provided food and lodging for the visiting team. The children received an outstanding education of the various areas while staying in Brussels and Amsterdam."

Doral's wife Connie stayed at home

in the 70's and was the Coordinator for the Family Services Program. In the 80's Connie taught 5th grade at Hahn Elementary School.

McKenzie, Keith

Keith served at Hahn from January 1984 - January 1988. This was no
t his first duty assignment.

Keith is another (of quite a few who shared the same AFSC as myself) 462 (2W1). He lived on base in the dorms for a while and also off base at Enkirch and Wahlenau.

At the end of his tour he returned to the States for reassignment.

His favorite memories are going to the winefests and meeting the locals. Worst memories include the foggy, rainy weather.

Keith went back to the States for vacation while stationed at Hahn.

McVicket,   David   &
Tawnya

Favorite   memories   here   include
"dancing at the N C O club until about
two and having breakfast with the best
fried potatoes." Worst memory - "the
pizza cheese that WOULD NOT melt."
They did not return home during the
years at Hahn.
They also report that "We were all
broke so we would invite each other to
our   houses   for   dinner   and   a   movie
(VHS). That year we watched When Harry
Met Sally 7 times. And had spaghetti a
lot."

Miner, Christine

Christine says that she arrived at Hahn as Christine Anderson and left as Christine Williamson. She arrived in 1984 for her first assignment and left in 1985.

Christine worked in personnel and lived in the dorm until she got married. She then moved to Laufersweiler.

Most favorite memories for Christine are: "All of my memories from Hahn are great, my favorite memory is that my son was born there. The commraderie of the folks stationed there was incredible - something I never experienced before or after. I loved the wine fests, picnics by the Mosel, visiting castles, riding down the Rhein watching fireworks from the castles on either side - the list just goes on and on."

She states that her worst memory is "leaving."

After completing the time at Hahn she left as a dependent wife. Her ex had orders to McClellan AFB, California.

She further states, "I loved every minute of my time at Hahn and on active duty. The only reason I got out of the Air Force was because we were working opposite 16 hour shifts and I was 8 months pregnant with nobody to watch our baby. I wish there had been other options but I know I made the right choice for my son."

Narvarez, Ruth

Ruth was at Hahn from 1982 - 1985 after having served at another assignment.. She was Ruth Crechard before she married.

She was a diet tech.

Traveling adventures while at Hahn included a trip to Holland.

Ruth says that her favorite memory was Christmas at the hospital. They had the dining hall decorated and had Santa come and give presents to the kids on anyone with dependent children.

Worst memory was that her husband had to go back to the States because of health issues. He passed away before she had a chance to get there.

Nemecek, Michael

After a previous assignment David arrived at Hahn in 1970. He stayed until 1971. During this year he lived in Neidweiller.

Michael's AFSC was 64570.

He traveled to the UK, Italy, France, Belgium, and Norway while there.

His best memories are the country and the German people. His worst memory is the lack of support for family of first termers which made life very difficult.

After leaving Hahn Michael returned to the States and was assigned to

England AFB, LA which was a real disappointment for him.

Nemeth, David

David's tour at Hahn, which was his first duty assignment, was from 2/82 – 2/84. He is another who shares an AFSC that I once had (462 –Weapons troop).

David says that he lived both on and off base. He resided, for a while, in Buch and Mastershousen.

His most favorite memories are, "Everything – the castles, and the people stationed there." He does not have any negative memories.

After leaving Hahn he returned to the States for reassignment. He also stated that he did not make a trip home during his stay at Hahn.

Norm

Norm was stationed at Hahn from 86 – 91 and says that he was stationed at another base before going to Hahn. His AFSC was 43171.

Norm's favorite memory is the personal connection between people and how everyone bonded.

Norm concludes by stating that Hahn was, "Rough and raw."

Olsen, Carl J.

After an assignment at Avon Park Bombing and Gunnery Range, Florida, Carl was assigned to Hahn in the year 1984. He stayed until 1990.

While at Hahn he lived off base at Punderich on the Mosel River. His AFSC was 81152.

Most favorite memories - "I worked Law Enforcement Flight, L.E. Staff Nco under CMSgt Powers with Debbie Asher and Marcy Hammes, and a stint as Confinement NCOIC and then in Law Enforcement Quality Control's New offices above the armory with the Col

Mike Wheeler. Wonderful people and a great assignment". His least favorite was the traffic accidents he investigated and the people who did not make it home.

After his assignment at Hahn he returned to Avon Park Bombing Range – a place he describes as, "Best kept secret in the Air Force."

Travel while at Hahn included trips to France, Luxemburg, Berlin, Sweden, Denmark, and a T D Y back to TyndallAFB, Florida for N C O Academy.

Otstot, Roger

Roger was at Hahn from November, 1973 through November, 1976, after having served at a prior location. He was a Ground Radio Communications Repairman, and lived in Dillendorf, Kirchberg, and Traben-Trarbach.

Roger's favorite memories include spending time with German friends. He worked with a German national who had children about Roger's age. They found him interesting and he thoroughly enjoyed spending weekends in local guesthouses and just learning about them and their families. He also enjoyed his travelling opportunities (Austria, France, Luxembourg, Sweden, Denmark, Holland, Norway, England, and Italy). His favorite trip was a trip to Berlin. He was able to go across Checkpoint Charlie and visit East Berlin.

His least favorite memory is the fog in the winter.

After leaving Hahn Roger returned to the States for reassignment.

Payne, Susan

Susan was at Hahn from May, 1983 until May 1987. She came to Hahn from Incirlik, Turkey. Her AFSC was 66170 (Logistics Plans).

Her favorite memories include wonderful German friends, the country side, and being on the Gunsmoke Team. Weather is at the top of her list of worst memories.

Susan says that she returned home once on emergency leave while stationed at HAHN.

She concludes by stating that Hahn was a great assignment. Her son was born there.

Potucek, Kenneth

Kenneth also had a longer than usual tour at Hahn. His dates of assignment are Sept. 1963 – July 1968. This would put Kenneth and me there together for at least part of the time. Like some of the others, Hahn was not a first assignment.

Kenneth was, like me, a 46250 which is a Weapons Loader. Being in the same career field, and there at some of the same time, it is really difficult to understand how I do not remember him.

A very important remembrance for Kenneth is that it was while at Hahn that his daughter was born. He also fondly remembers trips to Garmish and to Holland.

Kenneth also mentioned a couple of unpleasant things about his time at Hahn. He did not like the Lt. that he worked for while in the Loading Section in the 10th TFS. He also was not real excited about trips to Whellus.

Kenneth reports also that he did not make a trip home on leave while at Hahn.

He lived, while stationed at Hahn, in Rhaunen and Shoren. He travelled six times to Whellus and also had a three day TDY to France.

Proxmire, Keith

Keith was at Hahn from Dec. 82 – Dec. 85. This was his first duty assignment after school. He stated his AFSC as 47250.

Keith's favorite memories include, "Wrestling for the Base Team and helping coach at the High School, going to wind fests along the Mosel, getting lunch at the small Imbuss just off base (killer Currywurst).

Among his least favorite memories from Hahn he mentioned, "Working snow removal maintenance at night."

Keith is another who was able to travel home while at Hahn.

Purdy, Jonathan A.

Jonathan served at Hahn from May, 1977 to May 1979. He had served at another assignment before going to Hahn.

Jonathan was an Avionics Instrument Systems Technician (32551) while at Hahn who lived first in the hospital dorm, then up the hill from Rodelausen, then near Hirschfeld.

His favorite memories include

walking with roommates off base any time of the day Without feeling threatened. They would often walk in the fields and in the nearby forests, always taking a different route. He enjoyed many Volksmarches on Saturdays. He also enjoyed singing in the base chapel choirs, both Protestant and Catholic.

His worst memory is getting left at Bernkastle by the rec. center tour bus two weeks after arrival. He had to walk back to base guessing about the roads to take. Later the same thing happened for five of them in Mainz-Kastell. They took the train, bus, and taxi to get back to the base.

At the end of his tour he volunteered to stay another two years but when he got orders for Kingsley Field, he "Jumped at it!"

He concluded his remarks with, "Hahn AB and my temporary assignments from there were a highlight of my time in the Air Force. I learned a variety of systems besides mine on the F-4E and I was impressed with what little I got to see at the annual air shows. When I arrived, they were five months into the Tactical Maintenance System's second try at the base and we had apprentices to train, so everything went as planned."

Purvis, Jim

- Originally from Somerset, Ohio

- Joined Air Force in 1961, went to Aurora Air Force Base in Aurora Colorado for Technical training for Guided Missile maintenance.

- Transferred to Hahn Air Force base late 1961.

- Assigned to 496th wing - F102 Interceptor Jets

- Worked as Defense Missile Guidance Systems Technician

- CAFSC: 3115W

- Rotated back to the States in Dec. 1964 and Discharged

- While stationed at Hahn, I did part time work (volunteer) in the Base Photo Hobby shop

  o I managed that operation from 1962 until I left in 1964

  o Taught base personnel how to develop pictures from film and print their pictures.

  o Also helped many personnel in various picture skills.

- Spent the next 40 years in the Insurance business until my retirement in 2004.

  o Traveled extensively for J C Penney Insurance co., as well as AAA.

- Spent lot of my previous years as photographer while traveling around the world.

  o During the last 15 years I have been the team Photographer for local Professional Hockey team.

  o Many of my game action photos also appearing in local Newspaper as well as other on-line hockey sites

- Currently reside in Knoxville, TN (Retired) enjoying my Grandchildren.

  o Medical issues for both my wife and myself have been keeping us from doing much traveling at the present time

- Also run several web sites

  o http://www.kibbc.com - local Booster Club for the hockey team that I do photography for.

  o http://www.wknox.net - my own personal web site

  o http://www.wknox.net/pics/ - where I currently publish photos for home games for the hockey team I photograph

- Also Amateur Radio Operator (Ham Radio)

- Also have a special Hahn Vets forum at http://www.wknox.net/hahn/. Haven't promoted it much so it hasn't built up yet. Hope to see it grow in the future.

That's my story - just enjoying retirement as it is.

I wish you well on your book. If there is any thing else I can offer - just let me know.

Quartermass, Paul D.

Paul was at Hahn from 1988 until 1992. This was his last duty station before retiring.

He lists his AFSC(s) as 64770 and 90650(?).

Paul's favorite memories include "The food and singing in the Bars and Stripes, our American Barbershop Quartet." He says that his worst memory is having to deal with satellite T V (Sky) when he lived in Hundheim.

Ray, Charles

Jim,

These are a few stories from my two books, "Tales of a Wandering Man", which is my life story, and also in a book I entitled, "The Spirit of Hahn".

The Spirit of Hahn contains my memories of my life and other's memories at Hahn Air Base.

I was stationed at Hahn from March 1964 to September 1967 and again from June 1977 to Aug 1984. I retired at Hahn and remained working in the Audio Photo Club as Warehouseman through December 1984. So I have lots of life stories from Hahn. I was over at Bitburg for 4 years from Nov 1969 - Nov 1973.

I am a bit slow in completing each but both now have over 600 pages full of my stories and even hundreds more stories sent to me by other Hahnites for inclusion in my book.
Like I said, I have hundreds of stories like these already penned and waiting for a publisher...

We remember the 60s, others remember their time from the 70s 80s, and 90's, but, unless the person spent his time in a bar, they must have memories similar to these. It is sad though that things changed, the assignments differed, building numbers changed, even the Unit designations changed...ie MMS became part of EMS...I seem to have been there for most everything that occurred at Hahn...it is basically my home away from Home. I have returned to Hahn maybe 50 times since I retired.

In The Spirit of Hahn, I have 62 chapters. "Where we lived", "where we ate", "where we partied", "Why I Like Hahn". Photos albums of every Unit in the Hahn Phone Book and photos of nearly every building on Hahn. I have an album for every town surrounding Hahn. I was keeping track of Hahnites who passed on in a chapter entitled TAPS. I have all commanders listed in another chapter. It is a very detailed history but I was co-writing this book with a friend and she has since backed away from the project. I don't have her permission now to use her stories...she was a dependent. She and others told the Dependent side and I and others covered the Military side. Her Dad took my position in EMS when I moved up to Wing Safety. He was murdered in 2004. We wrote stories together and finally we just stopped.

Billy

First Memories of Hahn

I was green back then...fresh out of a small Texas town, Rosenberg...in 1963. Hahn was my first assignment after basic and tech school. We, (13 of us were in Munitions Tech School together at Lowery Air Force Base in Denver, Colorado and six of us went to Hahn and a 7th went out to Morbach) got off the Boeing 707 at Rhein Main Air Base from McGuire on march 26, 1964 and a short time later, we were on our way to a place called Hahn Air Base..

We took the Blue Goose and bounced in it for 4 hours. We crossed the river at Bingenbruck. We stopped for a break at a gasthaus just after Stromberg.

As the bus driver drove on, I wondered...like the kid in me still wonders....how much further....it is to this place called Hahn.

I remember it started getting foggy. And I couldn't figure out which direction I was heading. I was sure that we were going up the side of a mountain because my ears were popping. Finally, the bus driver slowed down and turned off B-327 and slowed our bouncing bus to a stop at the gate. It was the Koblenz Gate and the entrance to Hahn Air Base. I still couldn't see where I was but the fog seemed to be only as high as the middle of the bus window.

At the gate, we picked up Sgt. David L. York. I suppose he was there to escort us. He was a lot older than we were but only had 3 stripes.

I'll never forget the question I asked in amazement as I looked out the right window as we were passing Base

Ops some 300 yards away. My question was a real question and I wasn't trying to be funny and remember, it was really foggy. And remember, we had been going uphill in the fog for a long time.

I asked out loud, and everyone on that bus heard my question, "Sgt York, how did they get that Aircraft Carrier way up here on this mountain?" I even thought...maybe there are some locks like the Panama Canal has and that is how they did it.

There was no response at this time but David didn't forget my question.

As we drove on into the base, he told us "that is where you will be working" as he pointed to G-1 (701). That was where the 50th MMS Commander's Office was located.

Sometime later, after getting signed in to the 50th CAMRON and assigned to our dorm rooms, (I was assigned to room 301 in Barracks C-27 (327).), we were told to meet downstairs for a ride out to where we were going to work.

The fog we had seen earlier in the morning had lifted by this time so we could see where we were and what our surroundings looked like. Downstairs, we were picked up by A1C Gil Jernigan for our first trip out to the area where we would be working. He was escorting us out to G-15 (715) to meet the OIC for the Munitions Storage Area.

Over on the left now was Base Operations. Gil Jernigan made a big deal to stop and point out, "Airman Ray, there's Hahn's Aircraft Carrier." Man did I get ribbed after that. It was okay and I also laughed about my crazy mistake. You have to admit though that the flat top of that building sticking up out of the fog and that tall tower sticking up higher. I had never seen a Base Operations but I had seen the top of an Aircraft Carrier.

My First Day at Hahn.

Settled In

I was finally "in place" meaning

that I knew where I would be for the next 3 years. I had a small camera and the next morning I took several photos which are posted in the "Barracks 327" photo album. I remember that it was cold, wet, rainy, and snowy and just a plain bad day. Little did I know. This was an everyday thing at Hahn in the Spring.

I remember the first walk down the hill from barracks 327 to the Chow Hall for breakfast. I guess it was then that I knew I was going to like Hahn. I could see Idar Koph off in the distance. I didn't know the name of the hill at that time but I remember that I couldn't wait for the chance to go to the top of it.

Idar Koph would wait a few months. I spent some time getting used to being at my new home, learning the ropes at work, and studying my OJT lessons and Career Development Course. I spent a lot of time reading and answering the CDC questions and soon after sending in my final test, I was notified that I was now a 46150 Munitions Specialist, Ammo Troop.

So these were my first memories of Hahn.

Many years later when I was at Hahn in September or October of 2005, I climbed through a broken window in the rear of the building and went up to my old room and there was this key in the door lock...actually, there were several keys in the lock...well, one key came home with me and has been added to my Hahn souvenirs. Back in 1964, the door lock was the old type with a slot for a skeleton key. I lost my key but fashioned a key out of a stiff rubber coated wire and used it to open the old lock many times back in 1964. I also used it to open the doors for the other guys who had lost their keys. I still have that homemade skeleton key that I used way back then.

Road Signs In Germany

I hope you'll enjoy my story about my first day in Germany and the signs I encountered on the way to a place called Hahn.

I didn't study German, I didn't know at the time that some of my ancestors were German, and therefore, I didn't know one word of German. I'm not talking about crossover words like hamburger and beer. I also knew that getting to Hahn without being able to speak the language was going to be difficult if someone wasn't at the airport when we landed that knew German and could take us to Hahn.

Fortunately, the plane landed at Frankfurt and taxied over to the American side of the Frankfurt Airport. And also fortunately, there was the Hahn Shuttle Bus driver there to pick us up. He spoke German, he knew the directions, and he would deliver us to our destination on the Blue Goose.

I had heard an old saying, "When in Rome, do as the Romans do." This phrase

127

got me started so I thought, "When in Germany, do as the Germans do" and this included learning the language. I started right then trying to read the German signs and pronounce the words so the words coming out of my mouth would sound somewhat like German.

It was a cold wet day at the end of March 1964. I was on my way to my first permanent/semi-permanent home away from home. Just after the Blue Goose left Rhein Main for Hahn, I began noticing the different signs. I asked the driver to pronounce the name of the signs so I could write them down and memorize them. After all, when in Germany do as the Germans do." I was going to learn German fast. So when I saw the Ausfahrt sign about 4 miles from the Airport and he pronounced it, I snickered but didn't doubt his enunciation. After several miles, I was vocalizing the words on other signs and I am sure the bus driver was rolling over inside with laughter at my Texan accent.

I was having a good time.... Back in those days, there were only four miles of Autobahn that we drove on between Hahn and Frankfurt and that was the last 4 miles leading up to the Rhein Main gate so as we putted along slowly through the little villages, I got to see many signs.

Back then, we crossed the Rhine River at Bingenbruck and we drove B-50 through every little podunk town between Frankfurt and Hahn. It was a four hour trip. The roads were so narrow that our bus and another bus going the other way could only pass when one or the other pulled over to the edge of the road and stopped until the other bus passed.

During this trip, I often saw one little sign on the wrong side of the road which I remember reading. I was certain the writing said "fub ganger green links." When I repeated the words, the driver didn't understand. And the little sign was already long gone so I couldn't point to it. It actually read "Fuss Ganger Gehen Links" or "Pedestrians Walk On The Left".

Anyhow, I was learning German from reading the signs. As we drove on, I was writing the words down. I had a good list. The words began to get even funnier. I just couldn't shake the word Ausfahrt out of my mind.

I recently analyzed the word. When you take the root word Fahrt, and add the suffix ten, you get Fahrten, the word for trip. I know you can also say "reise" for trip as well. When you take the root words like Aus, Ein, Zu, Durch, and Hin and add the root word fahrt, you wind up with words that give directions like Ausfahrt, Exit; Einfahrt, Entrance; Zufahrt, Approach; Durchfahrt, Thoroughfare or drive through, and Hinfahrt, Driveway.

Well as we drove down those little winding roads, we came to a town with the little yellow sign with the name that ended with the word "Fahrt". So I asked the driver to pronounce the name of this town for me so I could write it down phonetically. He turned to me; I was sitting on the door side in the front seat, and said "Heidenfahrt".....I couldn't help myself....I laughed until we got into the fog at Hahn. I couldn't write it down. I am still laughing after 42 years. Hopefully, you are too.

If you land at Frankfurt, and take the Autobahn to Hahn you are sure to pass by the Heidenfahrt Tankstella. I usually try to stop and take a photo of the sign and my rental car....I needed the photos to prove my story to the doubters. I have two or three pictures here already.

In 1977, I heard my kids laughing about these words, too. As big as Germany is, I wonder if there really is a town named "Ausfahrt"! I know for sure that you can actually go to Heidenfahrt.

Dorm Life

I lived in the corner room on the 3rd floor of Building 327, room 301, overlooking the Airman's Club for 27 months. When Marlene and I got married in July 1966, she and I packed up my things from the barracks and moved out to Julius Wedertz's "Bergbitzerhof" Farm. The farm is located out by Emmeroth and Pilmeroth. Linda, his daughter still lives there on the farm.

Room Mates

I roomed with Jim Early, Weapons Maintenance, Thomas Gordon, Orderly Room Clerk, Richard Grizwold, "The Sheet" as Tom referred to him, who worked in Inspection with Jernigan, and then me, Billy Ray, Storage and Handling.

The Jell-O Flick

I have a Chow Hall Story. The 4 of us, Bob Curry, Bill Ford, Albert Payne, and Billy Ray (me), who were on the same alert crew got relieved for breakfast when the first 4 day shift personnel arrived at the Bomb Dump, G-15 gate. They sort of took over our shift responsibilities so we could go eat. As they were coming through the gate, we were going out.

When it came time for the noon meal, we went to lunch before everyone else and after we returned, we "held down the fort" until they returned after lunch.

This story occurred during the supper break (early chow at 3:30p.m.) before everyone else in the Bomb Dump left for the day....This was in 1964....so things are in perspective.....

Anyhow, we were in the chow hall and sitting at the table and finishing up our meals. We were all sitting there acting our ages when a very small piece of jell-o accidentally made its way off from the fork going into someone's mouth and fell onto the floor. I believe it was Bill's fork. He stopped and bent over and picked it up as any sensible, thoughtful young GI would do. As he tried to place it back onto the dinner plate, that little piece of jell-o got stuck like glue to his finger.

Yep...see where this is going? To get it off his finger he rubbed it against the plate and it stayed stuck to his finger. So he gave his finger a little flick at the plate...zing...off his finger it flew. That red jell-o caliber .40 projectile flew through the air hit Bob square between the eyes and stuck. Bob simply wiped it off with a dinner napkin and that should have been that. Trouble is, the rest of us we laughing so hard at this flicking of the sticky jell-o that we got others laughing with us.

In the meantime, Bob sat there not cracking a smile...being crew chief and setting a good example, he very casually cut a 1/4 inch piece of his sticky red jell-o and placed it carefully onto the end of his spoon handle. He then lifted the spoon for all to see, and carefully aimed it back at Bill. Bob's shot was a little off target and the volley meant for Bill hit Albert.

Now Albert was involved. Albert reciprocated and hit Bob in the chest with a spoon full of jell-o....I was just a bystander...eating away at my jell-o but laughing more than the rest. They were trying to keep a straight face while doing their dirty work and all were acting as if nothing else was happening....even though the entire chow hall was now looking at our table....that's when Bob took his block of rubbery and stickier than glue jell-o and placed it nonchalantly into my hat....I didn't see him do this deed but everyone else did...because everyone else busted out in a roar to beat the band.

As we were getting up to leave, I realized my hat was now heavier than when we first came in and I looked inside....there was Bob's jell-o in my hat.

I quickly came up with a short lived plan to rub it in Bob's hair. When he saw that I was about to put it someplace else other than back on the table, he wanted to be sure it wasn't in his hair so he grabbed my hat with the jell-o still in it.

I was trying to grab that sticky gob of jell-o out of my hat and between the two of us we managed to squish that jell-o into liquid right there inside my hat. We ruined my hat and laughed until we couldn't stand. Sitting there in the chairs we finally got our composure.

I'll bet there are those who were there that day, if it was during the 70's and 80's, who would have been ready to holler food fight...and who knows what may have happened after that but fortunately, that was as far out of control as we let our food fight of the 60's get. It was funny then and another good memory for now.

50 Munitions Division
Munitions Storage and Handling Section

I was a 461X0 Munitions Specialist. I was assigned to the 50 Munitions Division at Hahn. The name changed again to 50th Munitions Maintenance Squadron, and later the name became 350th Munitions Maintenance Squadron. We were responsible for storing and maintaining all the explosive munitions required to accomplish Hahn's overall mission.

I was stationed here from March 27, 1964 to September 15, 1967. I worked with the best bunch of guys. Our bosses were the best. Everyone was a willing participant.

For every job that came up, I never saw

anyone who was lazy toward job accomplishment. Someone always volunteered to take the job before the NCOIC had to assign the task to someone else.

I worked with SMS Willie S. Seabrooks, Lonnie Miller, George Steret, Faun M. Smith, Lt William Beardsley, David Wiebel, Brookman, Bob Curry, Bill Ford, Ed Thomas, Roy D. Falkner, Claude Westfall, Lt Richardson, Al Payne, Gil Gernigan, Richard Griswold, Dennis Finucan, Ron Stupka, Jim Bradley, Moss, Mathiesian, Smitty, Shorty, David York, Lee Paul, Joe Rollins, Larry Bounds, J.C. Smith, Jerry Tyra, Larry Bounds, Tom Showalter, Gary Raymond, Mike Navratil, Paul Christman, Stacy, Billy Burke, Brookman, Ernie Szocs, Larry Bowens, Paul Woedenhoeft, Rich, Michael Palmateer. Michael Pellitier, Mike Palmatier and a host of other guys.

There were already guys on the Alert Crew but I wanted to be one of the crew members. They worked 48 hours on duty and then had 48 hours off duty. I had to wait until one of them wanted to come back on day shift.

Letter to friends...Hahn Air Base 1964-1967
Written in 2004

I PCSd'd to Hahn after tech school and began my military career in Munitions when I was just 19. I worked in the Munitions Storage area. I lived up in the front corner room of Bldg-327 with Richard Grizwold, Tom Gordon, and Jim Early until July 1966.

I remember some of the guys from those days who were in old 50th Munitions Division. Some of those guys were given new Specialty Codes and they became 462X0s or Loaders. The rest of the guys remained as 461X0 Munitions Specialists. The loaders put the munitions on the Airplanes and the Munitions Handlers stored and maintained the munitions until they were needed.

The following are names of the guys I can remember who were stationed at Hahn during my 3 ½ years at Hahn. We all shared a milestone in our lives at Hahn. Bill Ford, Bob Curry, Claude Westfall, Al Payne, Lonnie Miller, Willie Seabrooks, Ron Stupka, Richard Griswold, Paul Woedenhaeft, David Wiebel, Jim Bradley, Moss, Matthusian, Gary Raymond, Smith, and Rodger Smith, David L. York, Larry Bowen, George Streret, Joe Rollins, Faun M. Smith, Gilbert Jernigan, Brookman, Mike Navratil, Dennis Finucan, Tom Showalter, Lt William Beardsley, Jim Early, Jerry Tyra, Lee Paul, and Darrell (Jack) Hall (Hall spoke German like I wish I could have and now can), Lt Richardson, Ernie Szocs.

Who was the guy that owned the Gray about 1950 Mercedes and ran with Brookman and Gernigan? I can almost say his name every time I get to this point but I just can't remember it.

There was Rich (red hair) and Dave, Tom Varga, Roy D. Falkner, Billy Burke, Stacy, Jesse Greer, John Thomas, Ed Thomas, and Paul Christman. These are the guys I worked with.

I'll bet if I could get up into Bldg 327, I could remember the rooms some of these guys were in. Some of the married guys lived in base housing.

I have a story for each of these guys. My stories about them are as vivid in my mind as they were when they happened. There is no time to tell them all here. I thank all of them for being part of my past.

Jim Early's Ray Charles Albums

Billy Burke melting down Jim Early's Ray Charles albums. He put several 33 RPM albums on the turnstile on the "record player" and forgot to turn the thing on. In the morning when the sun came up, it shined through the window and the heat caused all the albums to sag down to the turn table.

Boy was Jim upset. Billy Burke got to move out the next day. He moved across the hall to Stacy's room.

Cuckoo Clock

Shortly after arriving at Hahn, I just had to have one of those Cuckoo Clocks so I bought one, It cost $14.00. I took it to my room and hung it on the way over my bed. It was sounding off every 30 minutes. It didn't bother me but it bothered Jim. Jim threw brogans and shoes at that Cuckoo Clock all night. Fortunately, he never hit it. His shoes though left black marks all over the wall around the clock and the clock cuckooed on. The clock still hangs here in my dining room.

Alert Crew

I just remembered that back in 1964, there were eight of us sleeping in that room. There were four Munitions Handlers and four Munitions Loaders.

Back just before I got to Hahn in March 1964, the 50th Mun Divers of the

50th Munitions Squadron, stored, handled, and loaded all the munitions. During my first few weeks at Hahn, the rules changed and 461X0s did the storing and handling and 462X0s did all the loading. I do remember that I got to observe one of the last loads that the 461X0s did but I wasn't certified so I couldn't participate in the load but I was part of the 4-man team. The only part of the load that I was allowed to do was loading the ammo and charging the gun.

So anyhow, the standby loading crew also bunked with us. That way when the alert horn sounded, the four loaders would split into two teams and drive the first two weapons to the flight line and load them. The four of us, who were the Munitions Handlers, would get the keys, open the igloos, pull out the trailers and hook them to the hitches on the four trucks. After locking up the door, we drove the four trucks to the front gate and waited for the supervisors and the other Munitions Troops to arrive on the job. We would pass off the Igloo Keys to them and when instructed, we would convoy the weapons to the flight line with Air Police in front and at the rear.

Often times, the exercises would start just as we were going off on our two day breaks and we would have to remain on duty until the exercise was over. Now very often but sometimes, we would get lucky and get out of the gate just before the alert horn sounded and of course, we would simply keep going rather than return to duty. That night though, we would return for duty and exclaim, "We must have just missed the alert horn when we left the base!!!"

The Rest of the New Watch Story

A few weeks after I go to Germany, I was assigned to Alert Crew duty. One night, I took off my watch to wash my face with soap and water. I placed my watch up on the glass shelf above the sink. And while my face was soapy, someone came into the shower room and took my watch. Since I didn't see or hear anyone, I couldn't figure out where it went but one thing is sure, it was never seen by me again. And for the next 3 years, I always suspected one of the cops in the guard shack, just through the bathroom door, of taking my graduation watch.

Speaking of Nuclear Weapons

It's funny, but the whole time I was stationed at Hahn, and over at Bitburg as far as that goes, no one, in my circle of German friends, ever touched on the subject of Nukes. Whether they knew and kept quiet or didn't know anything at all will be a mystery. How many times each year did we deliver those things to the flight line under those tarps...What did they think was under them....Peanut Butter...in 2,000 pound bomb shaped containers covered with tarps?

When the Alarm whistle blew and the Germans were sent home, did the Workers think we were mad at them or maybe we just didn't want them to see the Peanut Butter Bombs? Oh, I am sure the German government knew what we had stored in those big igloos...they would surely have been "up tight" if they discovered that we stored them and they knew nothing.

The On Base, Wueschheim, Metro Tango, Morbach Storage Areas...It doesn't matter, the munitions, the bombs, and nukes stored there were there to show America's resolve to maintain a free and democratic Europe and to show strength to the Russians who knew they were there.

The Nuclear Weapons, Conventional Bombs, and Missiles that we stored and maintained at Hahn kept the peace. Whether it was one single Nuke or a million of those things, the peace was kept, the Cold War was won, and Russia finally collapsed and tore down that wall. Germany was once again reunited in Peace.

The fact that there have been so many wars and battles, since the wall fell, still boggles my mind. It seems, throughout the Cold War, the United States demonstrated how using strength in military might, coupled with Diplomacy and Friendship, goes a long way to preventing war. Why can't other nations simply do the same and stop all the bloodshed. We all know that some peoples don't fight for peace. Their wars and acts of terrorism are merely "their way of life."

Anyone of the protestors, who died protesting the American's presence, did so, from overdosing on drugs or alcohol or in a car or bus accident or by jumping in front of a driver who couldn't stop when they suddenly jumped into their car's path. No one died because of an American causing them physical harm.

Reed, Cynthia Vaughn

Cynthia was at Hahn twice. The first time was 1959 – 1962 and then again 1970 – 1974. She was there with her parents the first time. The second time was spent there with her husband. She states that she "Loved everything about being there, both times." She further states that she does not have any bad memories. She did not return home during either of her stays at Hahn. "Too expensive!" she says.

Riedel, Katherine Marie (Rabon)

Katherine was at Hahn from 18 Sept 78 to 15 Dec 1980. She was Katherine

Marie Rabon while at Hahn. It was not her first time at Hahn. Her AFSC was 43151. Favorite memories include Volksmarches, seeing all the beautiful churches, and Garmish. Her least favorite memory centers on working with some of the guys in her shop that were very negative about working with women. There were several women in the shop. Katherine did return home during her stay at Hahn.

Katherine lived in the dorms for a while but then moved off base. In addition to the countries listed on the survey she also visited Spain, France, and Austria.

Renniger, Harold J.

Harold's dates of service at Hahn are, Jan 64 - Aug 67. It was not his first assignment. His AFSC was 42173. Among favorite memories Harold says that he met his future wife while stationed at Hahn. He also enjoyed racing micro midgets. Winter weather is his worst memory.

Harold did return home once during his stay at Hahn.

In reference to his comment about meeting his wife at Hahn, he follows by saying, "Met my wife there, never had a date, married her and have been married for fifty years."

(Wow!! Not many folks can make that claim! CONGRATULATIONS HAROLD!!)

Ricciardi, Victor (Rick)

Rick served as a crew chief at Hahn from 1966 - 1967. It was a 1 year reassignment for him. He had previously been at Tinker AFB Transient Alert for the prior 6 months.

Rick lived in the barracks across from the Chow Hall. During his year at

Hahn he went TDY to Wheelus AB.

His favorite memory is stated as: "At the age of 18, the first time overseas, it was great. The best part was meeting, and living with other guys from all over the States."

His worst memory is the weather.

After leaving Hahn, he went to RAF Wethersfield for his final 2 years.

Since leaving Hahn he has tried to contact some of his old roommates. He had 3 of them that he's been searching for. Last year he got lucky and found one - Larry Johnson from L.A. Unfortunately he was terminally ill with cancer and could not communicate since being hospitalized. He did e-mail his wife who told him that he also had been searching for Rick all those years. Sadly he passed away 2 weeks after his initial contact.

Rod

Rod arrived at Hahn in 87 for his first duty assignment. He stayed until 1988.

He was a SP (81130) and lived on base. He returned home during this year at Hahn.

Rod's most favorite memory is the people. He has no unfavorable memories.

After leaving Hahn he returned to the States for discharge.

Sand, Gary

While many memories of Hahn involve gloomy weather, beautiful scenery, snapcaps, church bells, bratwurst, and Mosel wine, my Air Force job is what I most clearly recall.As a smaller tenant unit, the 586th TAC Missile Group is often forgotten when memories of Hahn AB are shared by those assigned to the host 50th TFW. The TM-61C Matador missile had been there in small numbers even before the 50th arrived, but our numbers increased substantially with the arrival of the TM-76A Mace in 1960. While the Matador was individually deployed on mobile launchers in the woods, as was the original Mace concept, we soon converted to a Rapid Fire Multiple Launch concept that placed eight missiles on alert at three hard launch sites spread around the countryside. Our missile sites were located some distance from the base, so many of the folks from our group headquarters and operations squadrons spent their on-base time sleeping and attending to squadron business. Most of our meals were eaten on site, or in the Metro Tango mess hall, so we didn't even have a big presence in the base consolidated mess at meal time.

About the only time the 50th noticed we were even there was when an exercise was called for all missile personnel. Someone from the 50 th with a sense of humor must have decided it would be good fun to notify the missile crews of an exercise by playing the old cavalry "charge" bugle call over the base PA system! It was always good for a lot of ribbing from the airplane people as we rushed from the barracks to our off-base sites.

From 1960 to 1963, I was a member of a Mace launch crew, tasked with performing a pre-launch test on a missile before turning it over to the launch officer. Like many other Air Force jobs, it consisted of hours of boredom, punctuated by moments of panic. One of those panic moments occurred during a winter rainstorm that had been raging for hours. Suddenly an indicator light began flashing on the launch control console that read: Booster Bottle Armed. That meant that the solid stage rocket motor that literally threw the missile off the launch pad had received a signal to arm...a situation that was supposed to occur just before an actual launch, not while sitting on alert status.

It was up to the special weapons tech to grab a PSM-6 meter and troubleshoot the system to see if it was indeed armed, or if it was only a false indication. Since a buddy was always required when working near the missile, I had the dubious pleasure of accompanying him out to the Junction Box that hung on the side of the missile launcher. It was the point where all the electrical cables from the blockhouse joined the missile and it was located about three feet from the rocket motor. Since static electricity could set it off, we had to shed our nylon parkas while troubleshooting. I'm not sure if my intense shaking was due to working in shirtsleeves in pouring rain at 35F, or fear of us becoming crispy critters if we touched the wrong pins in a connector! Fortunately, it was a false indication.

Another time of panic was when a crew was conducting an engine run on a missile. The procedure was to momentarily bring the jet engine to full throttle and then reduce it back to idle, but something went wrong and the engine would not throttle back and it would not shut down. It thought it was ready to head for some Eastern Bloc country and was trying it's best to get airborne! After a few minutes of runaway operation the blacktop behind the concrete blast pad began to melt and roll up like a carpet, blowing the underlying base gravel hundreds of feet behind the bird. Finally, one of the maintenance crew members was able to climb on the launcher, reach inside the missile, and manually close the fuel shutoff valve. The only damage done was

to the blacktop, and the Germans had
that repaired in a couple of days.

Though we were on alert when the Berlin
wall was erected, the most memorable
days of my thirty months at Hahn were
during the Cuban crisis in 1962. The
entire base was prepared for WWIII and
it was nearly a traffic jam with all of
Hahn's F-100s and F-102s constantly
flying missions. F-104s from a unit in
Spain were detached to the base, and a
pair of Starfighter interceptors with
missiles on the wings in place of fuel
tanks, would sit idling at the end of
the runway for some time, then return
to their area to refuel when another
pair relieved them. This went on around
the clock as the crisis became more and
more tense. Our launch crew was on duty
at the time the Soviet ships were being
intercepted by our Naval blockade. We
had been keeping our missiles at a
readiness stage that allowed them to be
launched within approximately five

minutes after receiving the coded launch order, and by all indications, it was an even bet that we would be doing exactly that. What was strange is that we were listening to AFN radio to get news of the confrontation. Except for frequent communications checks with the blockhouses, the bosses at higher headquarters were eerily silent. I can still feel the relief that prevailed when the Soviet ships turned around instead of challenging the blockade. I'm certain the general population had no idea how close we came to nuclear war that day.

Gary Sand
Ponder, TX

Gary was at Hahn in the early 1960's. He went to Hahn after a previous assignment.
His AFSC was 31453M and while at Hahn he lived both on base and off base in

Traben Trarbach.

Gary's best memories are visiting the small towns and enjoying the food, drinks, and festivals. His worst memory is the ORI's that seemed to never end.

At the end of his tour he returned home for discharge.

Saymon, Jay

Jay began his tour at Hahn in January, 1977 and saw it come to an end in December of 1978. It was not his first tour. He came to Hahn after his first assignment at Edwards AFB, California. His AFSC was 43151c – Aircraft Maintenance Specialist, 1 & 2 Engine Jets.

Jay's fondest memory is his landlord and his family. When he moved in they told him they would be his Mother and Father away from home. His worst memory is the long days spent in a cold Tab Vee.

Jay concludes with this statement: "Miss the area. Too bad I did not realize how great it was at the time."

Schmidt, Michael

Michael is a German civilian who was in the Hahn area from 86 - 91. During this time he lived in Buchenbeuren.

While at Hahn Michael was in charge of the React radio club. After leaving Hahn he moved to Munich to do construction work.

Michael traveled to Belgium, Netherlands, Luxembourg, and Denmark. He says that his best memory is his many American friends. He concluded his remarks by stating that he is, "Still searching for the guy who was in charge at Hahn Air Base during the mid-70s - late 70s."

Schnorf, Greg

Greg served at Hahn from 7/75 - 10/77 for his first tour of duty after basic and school. He worked in the Security Police area.

Greg says that his favorite memories were travelling around by train and walking in the forests. Being in the military is his worst memory. He did not return home during his stay at Hahn.

Greg comments that he wishes he had been older or at least more mature as he thinks he missed out on a lot from youthful foolishness.

Schubert, Robert (Bob)

Bob is another one who had more than one tour at Hahn. His first tour was from 79 - 81. The second tour was from 86 - 91. His first tour was not his first assignment after tech school.

Bob's AFSC was 43171 (Crew Chief).

His best memory is living in the local area (Kappel). Exercises was named as the worst memory.

Bob returned home once during his second tour at Hahn.

Shaffer, Tim

Tim was stationed at Hahn from Dec 1961 until Dec 1965. He went to Hahn after a stint in the Navy where he completed tech school (MG – 10 Weapons Control System). His AFSC was 32251. His most favorite memories include "Foggy weather, nights in German Gasthauser, opportunity to learn and practice German, travel opportunities around Europe. His least favorite memories include working the F 102 radar on the cold, windy flight line. Also listed as least favorite is living in the 496th barracks. Tim did not return home while stationed at Hahn.

Tim's travel opportunities were many.

In addition to all the countries listed on the survey he visited many others. He eventually returned to Germany (Ramstein, twice) but lived in the Hahn area (Budenbach) and commuted to Ramstein. After retirement from the Air Force he worked for a German construction company until 1985 when he contracted to run the S & S bookstore on Hahn. He remained in this position until he returned to the U S in 1991.

Sherrill, Mike

Memories of My Tour at Hahn AB, Germany

My journey began on Oct. 7, 1966, when my buddy Jim Martin and I left McGuire AFB and the good ole' US of A for a three year tour in Germany. We arrived at Rheine-Main AB, Germany on Oct. 8 after a long "across the big branch" flight. We processed in-country and arrived at Hahn on Oct. 9.

We were indoctrinated early as one of the "veterans" from the 10th TFS (our new home) carried us to glorious down town Lautzenhausen and introduced us to the drink of choice, German beer. Also viewed some of the local residents which included local girls with the Black Forest growing under their arms - Yech!!!!!!! Don't remember too much about that evening as the beer was served warm and was 15% alcohol. Probably was not a pretty picture.

Our squadron had been operating with the F-100 Super Sabre fighter but was being upgraded to the new F-4 Phantom and was phasing out the F-100's. There was a large influx of new troops coming in over the next several weeks and, when our squadron reached full strength, began forming into crews of 4 and training for certification on all the munitions loads carried on the Phantom. And there were a lot.

Everything from dumb bombs (unguided) to air-to-ground rockets, guided air-to air and air-to ground missiles, 20mm Gatling guns and various nuclear weapons.

I remember the feeling of excitement, nervousness, and awe at the responsibilities we were taking on. The fear of screwing up and letting your crew down was also there.

My crew was one of the last to get their chance to certify and I remember listening to all the stories from those ahead of me about what to expect, including many cuts and blisters. The F-4 was a knuckle buster to those of us having to reach in her mechanical bowels to attach various cables and arm the wing stations with munitions and explosive cartridges, I remember my friend Jim (the author of this book) wearing his dad's old jump boots from WWII and getting blisters on his toes

which became infected. I suffered
through blisters on both my knees (I
still have scars) and wore out the toes
of two sets of boots as well as the
knees on several pairs of fatigues
during the two week or so training
period needed to qualify as a Weapons
loader, Most of our time was spent on
our knees under the aircraft,

I well remember the cold, foggy
days and the feeling that the sun was
punishing us for leaving the good old
USA.

Being a NATO ally meant alert
exercises at base, wing, and full NATO
participation to insure a high level of
readiness as we were the first line of
defense against attack from the Soviet
bloc in Europe. We were told we were
only 7 minutes by air from the Russian
occupied border.

One of my most vivid memories

occurred on June 6, 1967. We had just
completed a mobility exercise which
included updating our worldwide shot
package and had returned to the
barracks late that afternoon when the
alert klaxon went off as well the song
"Tiger By The Tail" blaring over the
loudspeakers. Then a voice came on and
said "this is NOT an exercise". We
piled out of the barracks and into
whatever truck we could commandeer and
headed for our shop. I dove into the
back of a pickup full of our guys and
forgot I had a cigarette in my mouth.
My crew member Shep cussed and I
realized my cigarette had burned a hole
in his trouser leg and was burning him.
Thus began our introduction to
participation in preparedness for came
to be known as the Six Day War between
Israel and her Arab enemies,

The next several days were a blur of
loading munitions , downloading
munitions, uploading new munitions,

sleeping at our shop and eating at a field kitchen set up in a trailer just off our flight line, and for some of us, dealing with a raging fever from getting a plague shot during the mobility exercise the first day. Fortunately, we did not have to give Israel our support that time; they took care of business without our help, thank you very much.

The German food also brings back fond memories. The bratwurst (mit pomme frites and mayo), the jaeger schnitzel, Nino's great pizzas, Mmmmm my mouth waters just thinking' about it.

But , most of all, I feel blessed to have known a great bunch of guys who I still remember to this day -- guys like Jim Martin, Joe Otto, Charles (Shep) Shepard, Jim Hoffman, Frank Donovan. Ed Troxell, Les Cook, Ted Ogonowski , Jay Campbell, John Boegel, Jim Milius and all those I haven't listed but still think about when I see photos or think of times past. Would love to have a reunion with ya'll and share those times again.

I rotated stateside one month after Jim Martin in 1969. He had a little over 6 months left and was reassigned to a base in Florida (tuff job but somebody's gotta do it). When my orders came I had less than 6 months left and was given an "early out" (hate it guys).

Jim Martin went on to join the Air Guard and actually retired after an interesting history (read his book). I went home, back to school and got my degree from Auburn University. I am now a retired (sort of) Alabama redneck who loves it. War Eagle!

Siembab, Gary

Gary arrived at Hahn in July of

1969 and stayed until July 1972. This was his second assignment. He lists his AFSCs as 55151 and 70250.

Summer winefests are at the top of the list of favorite memories and leaving there to come back to the States is his worst memory.

Gary returned home once during December, 1971 so that grandparents could meet their new grandson.

Simon, Patrick J. (SSgt)

Patrick went to Hahn on Thanksgiving day 1969 and departed in January of 1973, for his first duty assignment after school. He lived in Barracks 327, room 308 for the whole time at Hahn and called it, "Home".

While at "Home" he travelled to Luxembourg, Denmark, Sweden, Austria, Switzerland, Italy, and Spain.

While at Hahn, Patrick was a 462

and worked in the 350th MMS. He was in the Weapons Release shop (Bldg. 1025) for the entirety of his stay at Hahn.

Patrick's many fond memories are as follows:

"Skiing the Zugspitze, Winefests, Bernkastel, Zell, Traben-Trarbach. Skiing in Italy, travelling to all the countries mentioned above, seing buildings that were over 1000 years old and still standing, meeting the girl who became my wife of 41 years, flying down the autobahn at over 100 miles an hour, bratwurst and Brotchen, Pommes frites, being invited to Christmas or thanksgiving meals with one of the married guys in our shop, and all the great friendships I made there."

In 1970 all of the planes were sent TDY while the flight line was resurfaced. He was assigned to Ramstein with one of the squadrons. It was at the conclusion of this TDY that he returned to the base. The day that the planes went back they all gathered on the roof of the barracks to watch their squadron fly in formation over the base just before they peeled off and landed individually

Patrick lists, as least favorite memories, "My first winter at Hahn (69). Supply had no parkas, no field jacket liners, no long johns. I froze working out on the flight line under those F-4s that first winter. Kneeling under those planes installing aft aero t/A missile launchers, in the cold/snowy/rainy/windy Hahn weather, while our fatigue pants were soaking up JP-4 off the tarmac. Riding back to the barracks from the shop (which was out by the Koblenz gate) on my Raleigh ten speed bicycle in a driving sideways rain." "I bought the Raleigh ten speed while at Hahn and rode it to and from Barracks 327 to our shop (Bldg. 1027) out by the back gate. I rode down the flight line access road to reach the MMS Barracks (327). My worst day on the bike was one night it was pouring down

172

rain, one of those sideways rains. When I got back I was completely soaked to the skin. I dumped water out of my boots. Even my wallet was soaked through. Worst bike ride ever!"

After completion of his tour at Hahn, Patrick returned to the States where he was reassigned to Forbes AFB in Topeka, Kansas as part of the traditional training program. He took the carpentry program there for six weeks and was discharged from there in march, 1973. He says that he didn't get into a carpentry field after that but learned sp,e skills that he still uses to this day from tha training. Looking back now, he says that "I should have stayed at Hahn." He thought at the time that he would need some skills to find work after leaving the AF and that was a program that was offered.

Patrick says that in Sept. of 1972 he used some leave time to return home to visit family and friends. He had been gone for three years and it was good to have gone home. Looking back now he says that he should have stayed at Hahn and better used leave to see more of Europe! It would have only been another six months. "Young and dumb!" he says. "Hindsight is 20/20."

Another interesting tidbit of information that Simon shared is:
"I arrived on at Hahn on a cold and damp Thanksgiving day in 1969. It was a dark snowy night and the trip took us on narrow winding two lane roads through several tiny villages along the route from Frankfurt to Hahn. It was snowing and the roads were somewhere between snow packed and slushy along the way. I remember the wipers on the bus going the whole trip. It was well after 19:00 hrs when the 'blue goose' pulled up to the Rec Center and dropped me off. I got directions from someone at the Rec Center on how to find the 350th MMS barracks, (327). He also told me how to find the CQ on duty once I

got there. I threw my duffel bag over my shoulder grabbed my B-4 bag and headed over and found the CQ on duty, just as I had been told. I told him who I was, that I had just arrived off the blue goose, and this was the squadron I was supposed to report to. He handed me two blankets, two sheets, and a pillowcase and had me sign for them. He then took me up to show me my room, (Rm 308, top floor just to the right of the latrine on the back side of the barracks). He told me that someone from the shop would contact me to let me know when to report there. He told me how to find the chow hall and left. Friday morning I was up early and waiting in the barracks to be picked up and taken to the shop. No one showed up. I spent Saturday and Sunday looking around the base figuring out where things were. Monday came and I waited for word, but again nothing. Tuesday, when I again heard nothing, I headed into the orderly room and talked to the airman behind the desk, telling him who I was and that I was told that someone would come to pick me up, when they were ready for me to go the shop, but that hadn't happened yet and I was wondering why. He took my name and went in to talk to the first sergeant. They both came back and the first sergeant again asked my name and service number. He then asked me where I had been the past three days and I told him I had been there since Thursday. He then said they had thought I was AWOL because I hadn't signed in. Apparently the CQ on duty on Thursday just assigned me sheets and a barracks room but had failed to sign me in. I was at the shop about 15 minutes later. That was my first couple days at Hahn."

Singleton, Joe

Joe's time at Hahn extended from

July 1977 until July 1981. It was not his first assignment. His AFSC was 75172.

Winefests, Oktoberfest, and Volksmarching are listed as favorite memories. An ex-wife and snow are said to be his worst memories.

Joe made a return trip to the States while stationed at Hahn. Joe says that, "Despite some marital problems, Hahn was the best 4 years of my 28 year career…best friends, best experiences, best job, and Germany is just a wonderful place, especially the Hunsruck!"

Slay, Jerry D.

Jerry was stationed at Hahn from Sept 1959 – August 1960. Hahn was his first duty assignment after tech school.

While at Hahn his AFSC was 56450.

This identifier is for a Plumber. (He received some skills which were very helpful after his many years in the Air Force. He retired as a SMSgt.)

Among his most favorable memories Jerry states "learning something of their culture and language. I enjoyed when I was honored with an invitation to their homes."

Jerry mentioned, as an unpleasant memory that he was "selected to go TDY to Dreux AB, France, for 60 days before I even completed a year at Hahn. After two weeks back to Hahn, I was given PCS orders back to Dreux where I stayed for 2 years."

Jerry did not return home during his tenure at Hahn.

He concludes with, "I was stationed at Sembach AB (1968-72) and back to Germany again at Spangdahlem (1976-79). In 1979, I went for a visit to Hahn and met some of the same German civilians I had worked with 20 years earlier. They acted as pleased to see me as I was them."

Smith, Joseph Eric

Joseph was at Hahn from Feb. 81 – Feb. 83. This was his first duty assignment after tech school. His AFSC was 53151.

While at Hahn Joseph lived both on and off base. He lived in buildings 326, 327 and 310. He also lived in Kiamt on the Mosel across from Zell, on the top floor of the Hershfeld Bonhoff, and in Reil on the Mosel.

He was able to travel to Luxemburg while at Hahn.

His most favorite memories are," My 1972 BMW 3.OSI and Octoberfest in 1982. Also all the winefests." Least favorite memories are, "Drunk and acting a fool on more than one occasion."

After Hahn he returned to the States for reassignment.

Joseph returned home on leave for 28 days in May of '81. He says that he "hopped over and back for $20." (Those were the good old days indeed!)

Smith, Michael

Michael was stationed at Hahn from March, 1985 through September, 1987. Hahn was his first duty assignment after tech school. While at Hahn, Michael worked as a jet engine technician. As for favorite memories he states "all the various festivals throughout the year." His least favorite memories, like many others, was "winter and NATO chem warfare gear." He did not return to his home until his tour was over at Hahn.

Stiles, Kevin

After serving at other assignments Kevin went to Hahn in Oct, 1990 and stayed through July, 1993.During this time he livedon base for part of the time and also in Neiderweiler.

Kevin's AFSC was 3P072A (Security Police/K-9 Handler) 50th SPS. Kevin deployed from Hahn during the Gulf War to Israel.

His best memory is country line dancing at the NCO Club. He enjoyed it every Wednesday evening.

After tour completion at Hahn, Kevin was reassigned to McConnell AFB, Kansas.

Strack, John "Jack"

John was at HAB from Jan, 1988 – Jan, 1990. Hahn was not his first duty assignment.

His AFSC was 81172A which is Law Enforcement Specialist Military Working Dog Trainer.

Among his many favorite memories John lists, "I suppose one of my favorites was taking 2 dog teams and himself with a bomb dog to Bitburg for a K9 Competition and winning or placing in the top 3 of each event we entered. This event was featured in an article for the Hahn Hawk." Congratulations Jack!!

His least favorite memory is the freezing cold nights on training exercises.

John is another member who did not return home while stationed at Hahn.

John says that of his 10 years in the Air Force his three years at Hahn were the best.

Spurgeon, Gary

Gary served at Hahn after another assignment in the 586th Missile Maintenance Squadron. His daughter was born on base while at Hahn. Gary enjoyed playing golf, basketball, softball, and all recreational activities. His least favorite memory was K P duty. He did not return home during his stay at Hahn. Gary says that he has many fond memories of experiences at Hahn.

Talvan, John

John spent the years 68-73 at Hahn after having served at a previous assignment. His AFSC was 98150 and he lived on base.

While at Hahn John traveled to Holland, Belgium, Luxemburg, Denmark, Spain, England, France, Sweden, Austria, and Italy. He also returned home once during his lengthy stay at Hahn.

Favorite memories for John include winefests and traveling to all the countries. His worst memory is the cold foggy winters.

After Hahn John went to Dyess AFB.

John stayed at Hahn for 5 years because, as he says, "I really liked being in Germany. I did learn the languaue and I have been back 7 or 8 times."

Taylor, Jim

Jim was assigned to Hahn from 79 through 81 and says that it was not his first duty assignment. His AFSC was 322x2b (sensors). His most favorite memory was riding his bicycle up and down the Mosel River. The weather and exercises were his least favorite memories. Jim returned home in 1980 on emergency leave.

Travel enjoyment while at Hahn extended to Turkey, Spain, England, France, Luxemburg, Austria, Switzerland, and Denmark.

Tharp, Jonathan

Jonathan arrived at Hahn in Nov 74 and stayed until Nov 76. It was not his first duty assignment after school.

Jonathan was a 23420 (Jet Engine Mechanic) and lived on base while at Hahn.

Travel stops for Jonathan included Belgium, France, and Spain.

His most favorite memories from his experience at Hahn are, "Touring the countryside which included the wine fests from Coken to Bern Kastel Ques on the mosel river. Attending a spiessbraten fest in Ider Oberstein, Touring the Pilar and makets in Zaragoza Spain. Attending the Spanish grand prix and seeing the newly elected King Don Juan Carlos. Partying with and making many friends from within the 50th FMS."

Least favorite memories are, "The food in the chow hall. Disorderly conduct at the Gasthauses in Lautzenhausen." Leaving."

At the end of his stay at Hahn he returned to the States for reassignment to the 378th FMS in Wurtsmith, MI.

Tom

Tom was at Hahn from 89 – 92 and

lived off base while there. It was not his first duty station. His AFSV was 81172.

While at Hahn he travelled to France, Belgium, Lichtenstein, Italy, Switzerland, and Austria.

He mentioned, as favorite memories, travel, scenery, food, and living on the economy. His least favorite memory is LSNs.

After completion of his service at Hahn, Tom was reassigned to another overseas base.

Turner, Rita Christine

Rita was stationed at Hahn from July 1989 – 1992 after a previous assignment. She was a Civil Service employee with Hahn Elementary School from 1989 – 1991. From 1992 until base closure she was with the Hahn hospital. She was not only Civil Service but was also a military spouse as well as an

Army Reservist.

While at Hahn she travelled to Holland, Poland, France, Luxembourg, Switzerland, Italy, Czech Republic, and Canary Islands.

At Hahn she lived in Sohren Base housing, Simmern Base housing, and Wallanau.

Great times for Rita include: Volksmarches. They volksmarched every weekend they were in Germany. Even when they were on holiday they volksmarched at nearby towns. Halfway they would grab a beer, and take in the beauty of the surroundings. They saw things one would never see such as a German bunker out in the middle of the forest, hidden away by overgrowth and time. They loved to try new foods on volksmarches such as the Pumpernickel sandwich that she thought had cheese/butter spread but was lard. She found that out after she ate it.

Least favorite memories are: "The sound of planes taking off and flying over Base Housing on Christmas Day with our troops headed to the Persian Gulf for the first Gulf War. My husband was on one of them. Sent chills through me. It still does. I'll never forget that morning. (2nd) Spent the last 3 months of my pregnancy at the Frauen Klinic at Mainz. The Hahn Hospital could not support my medical condition. I learned allot of German there since English was limited. No TV or radio. Read lots of books. Very lonely."

After Hahn's closure they were reassigned to Spangdalem for another 4 years. They did not go home for a visit after Hahn but rather opted for the Canary Islands. That was back when you had the option to return home, at government expense or go elsewhere.

Rita concludes by stating that her years at Hahn were the happiest years of her life.

Vedas, Richard (Dick)

Dick went to Hahn in May of 1965

and stayed until 1968. He describes himself as a "barracks rat." He had previously been assigned to Hamilton AFB, CA from 1961 – April, 1965 where he worked as an A & E radar Tech on F-101B's. His AFSC at Hahn was 32271H (Weapons Control Computer Specialist) on Radar for F-102's with the 496th FIS.

While at Hahn he traveled to Belgium, France Netherlands, Austria, Spain, Italy, Denmark, and Sweden.

His worst memory is "Being diverted from 32nd FIS at Soesterberg and assigned to the 496th at Hahn, and then being sent TDY to the 32nd to train 3 levels for 120 days."

After his time at Hahn, Dick returned to the States to the 322nd FIS at Kingsley Field in May, '68. He got out in Oct '68.

Walsh IV, John F.

After a previous assignment, John

served at Hahn from May 86 to May 90. He lived on base for part of the time and also lived in Kirchberg. His AFSC was 42191.

While at Hahn John traveled to Turkey, Spain, Italy, France, Morrocco, Israel, England, Belgium, Netherlands, and Luxembourg. He did not return home during his tour at Hahn.

His best memory while at Hahn is the TDY's. Worst memories include twelve hour (plus) shifts playing war games in full chem. gear.

After leaving Hahn John returned to the States for reassignment to Hector Field in Fargo, ND as an Air Force Technical Advisor to the Air Guard.

Ward, Jim

Jim was stationed at Hahn from Oct. 87 - Oct. 90 after serving at other bases. He lived both on and off base during these years. His off base home was in Kleinich.

Jim was a 46170 Munitions troop at Hahn and lists as favorite memories, "Towns along the Mosel, and local village festivals." His least favorite are Nato TAC Evals.

At the end of his stay at Hahn he returned to the States for reassignment.

Ward, Vernon

Vernon was stationed at Hahn from 11/1967 – 9/1969 after a previous assignment. He lived in the barracks while at Hahn. His AFSC was J32570A.

While at Hahn Vernon traveled to Luxembourg, Belgium, Holland, and Libya. He returned home for Christmas in 1968.

His favorite memory is winning slot machine jackpots at the Airmen's Club while his worst one is the day to day boredom due to a light workload caused by poor flying weather.

When Vernon completed his tour at Hahn he returned to the States for discharge. He says that he volunteered for every TDY assignment away from Hahn that he could. To him, Hahn was a good place for married personnel and families but not so good for many young, single folks.

Warner (Bobos), Janet

Janet was at Hahn from 1/3/1981 to 6/25/1983. She was Janet Bobos until she married a SP and became Janet Warner. It was her first duty assignment. Janet was a cook (62230). She worked in Victor Alert and Zulu barns where she says she spent most of her time.

Her favorite memories are, "Wine pig fests, volksmarches, food and people."

Also among favorites are: "Meeting my

husband at the bowling alley getting married in Kirschburg, having my first child... volks marching wine festival ling my daughter be baptized by a bishop in the town where we lived they ring the bells and the townspeople came to witness the baptism fasching, Munich the Oktoberfest traveling through Europe and the wonderful food and people and friendships."

She lists, as her worst memory, "Chemicals during exercises."

Janet also stated that her time at Hahn was, "The best times of my life ...unforgettable, made me who I am today."

Janet travelled to Holland, France, and Luxembourg while at Hahn.

After serving at Hahn she was "Sent to Grand Forks North Dakota. It lasted only seven months. We were gonna reenlist but was told we had to do five years there. We wanted to go back to Germany and they told us no. Therefore we did not reenlist but we got out and became civilians. My husband threw away nine years of military service because of that assignment Hahn which really ruined us.. Grand Forks was not a nice base, it was horrible. Everybody was for himself; the friendship wasn't there There was nothing to do but fish and hunt.

Weideman, Mark

Mark arrived straight from tech school in July, 1983 and stayed until 1986. He was a security policeman. He lived off base in Soren.

Mark's good memories are skiing in the Alps and the many wine fests. He says that he does not have any bad memories.

While at Hahn, Mark traveled to Austria, France, Spain, and Amsterdam. He also returned home during his stay at Hahn.

Welch, Dana

Dana was at Hahn from June of 1978 to May/June of 1981. She says that among her favorite memories are "Travelling with the swim team, Brochen rolls, kinder eggs, sledding, German friends."

Among least favorite things she says, "Missing McDonalds, ha! I was just a kid!"

Dana did not return home during her stay at Hahn.

In addition to the above, Dana shares that she was a dependent child, ages 7-10 while at Hahn. While there she was a Girl Scout and was on the Hahn Seahawks swim team. She remembers that her favorite meets were in Belgium and in Berlin. They got to ride the train there which she says, "Was so cool!"

Another great memory was that she had a German friend who lived across the street.

Wellman, Dennis

Dennis went to Hahn in 75 and stayed until 77. It was not a first duty assignment for him. His AFSC was 43250. While at Hahn he lived on base.

Dennis traveled while at Hahn to Austria, Luxemburg, France, and Spain.

Dennis says that his most favorite memories are: "Friends, sightseeing, winefests, Oktoberfest, Faushing, Traben-Trabach, and Cochem." Least favorite are the fog and freezing rain.

After his time at Hahn, Dennis returned to the States for discharge.

Wheaton, Ronald

I was stationed at Hahn '64 until
October '66. My first few months were
spent living in barracks and then when
my wife joined me we lived on a farm in
Ebscheid. I did not return home during
this time.

There were about 29 of us who
controlled the Fuel on base. Jet fuel,
Mo-gas,Av-gas. (115/145)

I refueled many jets and copters and
recips for all squadrons including the
496th and the Metro-Tango areas behind
fences. And some Missiles off base
because they were powered by old jet
engines using JP-4.

I have many stories but will reserve
them for a future venue.
One bad memory was seeing a gang of Air
Police attacking people in the Dolly
Bar.

I am in touch with a few of my old POL pals to this day living in many different states. I returned to Virginia and the first job I had was at National Airport refueling planes. My most memorable experience there was sitting on top of my truck watching as Washington Dc burned due to the King Assassination.

It reminded me of that movie Gone with the Wind when they burned Atlanta. A sad day!

Some of those pics are INSIDE our barracks. We lived usually 8 to a room divided by our lockers.

One is in front of the Refueling control building.

One   is   our   big   orange   truck.

In 1965 we had ORANGE Baseball hats
with Black POL and soon after we
switched to BLACK HATS with white POL
logo. (Petroleum)

One is of the Decals I saved from HAHN
to place on the back window of our
cars.

I still have two left and another is of
the GLASSES I saved from Sgt Talerico's
NCO club.

Good luck with your project and if I find anything else I will send them to you.

Kind Regards and God Bless,

Formerly Sgt. Ronald Wheaton. 3 stripes was Airman First Class then when we did our 2 year stint after the four active duty they called it SGT.? Go figure.

When I was at Hahn 4 strippers were STAFF SGT.

Ronald Wheaton

Ps My wife and our old VW BUG at a football game for Hahn Hawks.

The BUG was our favorite vehicle hack then. We also had a Peugeot which I wrecked following a HONEY WAGON one day that was leaking it's good all over the road. Our local farmer came and got me and towed me back to Ebscheid where all the kids stood on the side of the road cheering as the Stupid

Amercan GI was towed home sitting on the hood of his car--yep-ME-

Woodell, Scott

Scott was at Hahn from Dec, 1988 to Jan 1992. He came to Hahn from another assignment. Scott was a Security Forces member and lived on base.

Best memories are wine festivals and Octoberfest. His worst memory is Salty Nations.

His travelling experience while in Europe include France, England, Netherlands, and Austria.
After departing Hahn Scot returned to the States for discharge.

He says that Hahn was his best assignment and that it was sad to see it shut down.

* *

* *

From one particular social media post the following are listed. They will be anonymously presented since only a couple of them have stated that they did not mind being identified. Where applicable they will be identified. The initial post had to do with a general statement regarding whether people actually "liked" their time at Hahn.

One respondent stated that he thought it was okay while there but didn't what he had until he ended up in Oklahoma and missed it.

Linda Giezentanner Larson stated that those who said they loved their time at Hahn immersed themselves in the culture and took many day trips and weekend trips to explore everything that was offered. She stated that she loved her time at Hahn.

Another respondent stated that they absolutely loved it. Every weekend they went to a different town to Volksmarch. They were able to see places that one would never see from a car.

Jennifer Hockley says that her parents LOVED their time at Hahn. Her dad said that people that didn't enjoy their time at Hahn were the ones who stayed in the barracks and pouted.

Jennifer further states that her mom and dad essentially had a yearlong honeymoon living in and near Hahn. In addition they brought home a very cool 1969 VW Beetle.

Jennifer continues with another memory. There was a guy that would come noisily into the barracks in the early morning "two sheets to the wind." (That was PURE Rod Hockley) Her dad and some of the guys finally got fed up with this, so the next time it happened they took matters into their own hands. It was the middle of winter, hence, snow. When the noisy guy came in and passed out on his bed, they picked up his rack and took it out in the snow. Needless to say, Noisy guy was quieter when coming in from imbibing.

Another lady says that they had the time of their lives!! There was so much to see and do! They spent twenty years in the Air Force and Hahn was their best assignment. They still miss being there today. She recently found the group on Facebook and was so excited to re-connect with old friends, co-workers and see pictures of what it looks like now. "Wow! What a shame to see how bad the place looks!"

One gentleman states that his time at Hahn was the most memorable time he/they had. They were to be there for much longer than they were. Even with the loss of their son and having to do a humanitarian reassignment it was still, by an astronomical distance, the best assignment they had. They love going back to visit. They are heading that way for a month and a half visit this summer. They are excited about staying in Cochem again.

Yelonda Lace Johnston shares that she was stationed at Hahn with her ex-husband from 1986 60 1990 and that they absolutely loved it. Her son was born at Hahn in 1986. Her ex-husband was with CES and passed away August 12th, 2012, at the age of 48 of lung cancer and throat cancer that spread to his spine. She states that Hahn was "great". She remembers outside of the base exchange the baked potato stand (it was awesome), and the pizza place on base that had ice cream (yummy!)

Another gentleman responded by stating that after he got to Hahn that he took a crash course in German. Work schedule was 2 days on, 2 days off, etc. Several of them would jump in the yellow VW beetle and just drive off somewhere, speaking English only when

they had to. Stopping in Guesthouses,
the Germans treated them like family.
With the winefests, beerfests,
exploring caves, castles, and forests –
it wasn't exactly that Hahn was great,
but the surrounding area was fabulous.

Other Miscellaneous Photos

From Janice Olson, entitled Hahn AB Oral Surgery (1977)

Janice was a dependent wife who was a Civil Service employee in the dental assistant position.

More from Janice Olson

Here I am, 2nd from left, w/ wine in my
hand and a song in my heart. Dig those
glasses! **Nancy Skog**, is that OK w/ you?
She's 2nd from the right, looking
mighty happy and relaxed. I don't
recall the names of the other two. The

one of the far right is Nancy's sister.
The date was around '77-'78 at some
German winefest down on either the
Rhine or Mosel. Ah...those were the
days, weren't they?

Another pic from Janice Olson.
Taken at Fairchild AFB Dental Clinic,
1975. They were in dental asst.
training. Pre-Hahn

Karen Randall, Lt. Col /Don Holliday,& me, Janice (Olson) Prouty.

 **From**

Richard Vedas

Miscellaneous picture of the base from mid-60's

From Capt. Doral (Butch) & Wife Connie McGee

Easter, 1 970.
Conniem
 Trina,Derek at
 Blankenroth,
 Germany

Top left - Volksmarch picture from 1984
with Doral (Butch) McGee, Wife, Connie,
and youngest child, Elina, who was born
at Hahn.

Butch and son, Derek, 1969

Connie's passport picture (1970)

Butch and
children

213

Top Butch with Trina and Derek in their
lederhosen visiting a castle ruin.

Bottom - AWAG (German American Ladies
Club) Urusual Graham and Connie McGee
with German ladies

Michael Ambrose shares the following information, including pictures from Wheelus AB, Libya from the late 1960's. Many who served at Hahn and have contributed articles for inclusion in this book, (myself included) made a trip (or possibly several trips) to Wheelus.

Here are his comments:

"Here are the only pictures I have of our deployment
to Wheelus. Almost half ot the 50th Air Police Squadron
was loaded on a C-130, along with other Air
Police Squadrons, from, I think England and Ramstein, and the next morning we landed in Wheelus Air Base.

As I remember it was due to the 6 day war between Israel and Egypt. Evacuations of non-essential personnel including dependents were held because of the media stating that the planes which bombed Cairo came from Wheelus.

There is not a lot regarding this event on the current internet data bases but I did find some. Lots of pictures are available of Wheelus on the internet also. I did send a picture of the propeller of the Lady Be Good (second picture, on the top, right) which has an interesting story. Info is available on the internet. (Interesting indeed!! I would greatly encourage the reader to check it out!)

Sorry I could not be more helpful. During my time in the military (July 66 – July 70) we never took a lot of pictures. Too expensive to develop.

217

From Patrick Simon

Flight of F-4's returning from Ramstein after TDY there while flight line was being resurfaced at Hahn

On top of barracks watching F-4s return
from Ramstein. (L-R) Leland Law, Barry
Hoke, Kenny (Cheeks) Black, Chuck
Picket, Pat Simon, Rich Bartlett.

From Jerry Slay

Jerry as a much younger man

F-102's

Base Chapel

From Kenneth Potucek

I bought this hat at Hahn in 1964 or 65 to keep my pins on. I lost it on a Lake in Oregon upon

 my return in 1966. The Church that I belong to in Tucson Az. Was having a yard sale in 2006 and this hat fell out of a bag that I was unpacking. 40 years and 1200 miles from where I lost it. The pins were still on the hat.

From Karen Hockley (Wife of Rod Hockley who was a room-
mate of mine
and fellow band
member)

At Wheelus Ab, Libya -- Brian Kruger & Rod Hockley

(2nd and 3rd from left

Rod Hockley on beach at Wheelus AB

222

From Karen Hockley

Wheelus AB, Libya

L to R) Ted Ogonowski, Jim Engle, Brian Kruger

C-124 "Gooney Bird"

223

From Karen Hockley

Load crew preparing for missile load

Enjoying Off-time   Jim Milius and Rod Hockley

Fun in the Barracks (front to back) Rod Hockley, Les Cook, Frank Donovan

224

From Karen Hockley

Rod Hockley the Cowboy

Outside our shop - moving weapons

Weapons display at Hahn

Former Room-mate - Joe Otto

Inspection in front of 10th TFS Barracks

Party time in front of 10th TFS Barracks

227

From Janice Olson   (Pgs. 228,229,230)

From left to right -- Brian Jacobus,
Col. J.P. Morgan & Tom Tom Hilton. Hahn
AB, Germany, late 1970s. Col Morgan was
our Base Dental Surgeon. — with Brian
Jacobus, Col. J.P. Morgan, Ken Miller,
tommy pants and Tom Tom Hilton at
Flugplatz Hahn.
Dr. Timothy J. Weaver (foreground &
currently residing in Edmonds, WA),
Sheila Johns, Dr. Richard Jackson
(currently residing in CA), Dr.
Hoerath, Dr. Savage at Hahn Dental
Clinic. Late 70s, I believe. Photo
compliments of Dr. Kenny Miller,
currently residing in GA. — with Tim
Weaver at Hahn AB, Germany

Dr. Timothy J. Weaver (foreground & currently residing in Edmonds, WA), Sheila Johns, Dr. Richard Jackson (currently residing in CA), Dr. Hoerath, Dr. Savage at Hahn Dental Clinic. Late 70s, I believe. Photo compliments of Dr. Kenny Miller, currently residing in GA. — with Tim Weaver at Hahn AB, Germany.

Hahn AB Dental Clinic, Oral Surgery Department. Dr. Timothy J. Weaver, Janice ("Nurse Jan") Olson (Prouty then, '77-'79 at Hahn) & Dr. Richard Jackson. Photo taken at our small Hahn AB Dental Clinic 23 yr. reunion. 2002 Edmonds, WA. — with Tim Weaver, Ken Miller, Hahn AB Hospital, tommy pants, Brian Jacobus, Richard Jackson and Hahn Air

Base Dental Clinic Staff, '77-'79. in
Edmonds, Washington.

Nurse Jan (Janice Prouty
Olson) and Dr. Richard Jackson. Mini
Hahn AB 23 yr. reunion, 1-18-02,
Edmonds, WA. We worked together in oral
surgery at the Hahn AB Dental Clinic. I
was there from '77-'79. — with Tim
Weaver, Brian Jacobus, Ken Miller, Hahn
AB Hospital, Tom Hilton, Hahn Dental
People 1979-81., Tim Weaver, Richard
Jackson.

From Richard Deupree

1977 Time Frame

Hahn Golf Course(possibly the second hole)

Patrick Simon shares an interesting story regarding his experience at the Hahn Golf Course. He says that he played a couple of rounds during the 69 - 73 timeframe. One memory was that he was playing after it had rained pretty hard. The grass and greens were really wet and soft. He was on one of the first holes, which ran right along the road heading to the clubhouse, He hit a 9 iron into the green and thought that he must have completely overshot the green as he did not see the ball bounce. When he got up to the green he found that the ball had stuck right where it hit and was half buried in the green. He picked up his ball, repaired the ball mark and putted out.

Another great memory from Patrick relates to the time they were laying in a group ahead of two, one of which had only one arm. Patrick states that it was, "amazing to watch him play. I don't know how but it had to take a lot of concentration to play with one arm." Patrick concludes with, "I remember I was really impressed at how far and straight he hit the ball."

Another note from Patrick is that Hahn is the first and only place he ever bought golf balls. He grew up across the street from a golf course and golf balls turned up in his yard on a regular basis. Golfers would hook them over the road and either not come and get them, or not find them when they did. In order to play golf at Hahn he bought two sleeves of balls. One of them actually made it to his home in his hold baggage when he left Hahn.

Richard Deupree

1978 I think...we were introduced to the replacement for the F-4. It was flown in and did a couple of fly-bys before landing. I remember thinking the F-16 was the sexiest aircraft I had ever seen!!!

This was flown into Hahn as an intro prior to Hahn receiving F-16's in early 1980's. F-4's transitioned out of

Hahn in '81 - '82 timeframe.

Picture shared by Richard Deupree

Picture posted on Facebook with the caption, "Two of the best years of my life"

Many responded with comments as indicated on following page.

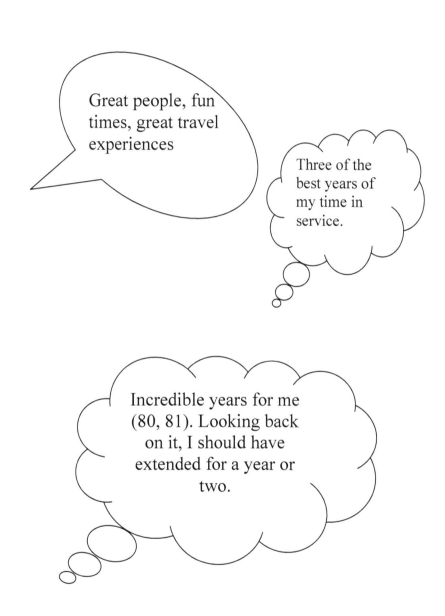

Great people, fun times, great travel experiences

Three of the best years of my time in service.

Incredible years for me (80, 81). Looking back on it, I should have extended for a year or two.

Pictures from Joe

Otto

Missile Loading operation

Shep, "supervising" from

interesting position

Mike, Shep, and Joe

Fun times!!

Mike,
Joe,
Jim, & Shep receiving training on gun

Idar Oberstein

Top Rt.- Ed Troxel, Top Left - Ronnie Morris,

Bottom Rt. _ Unknown, Bottom Left - Jim Martin

THE ZARA'S . . . Hahn's popular band, the Zara's, will be one of five bands which will play throughout the 12-hour show. Other bands came from Germany, Spain and Holland.

The Zaras

Played often at Hahn

The Mosel Valley Boys – Sonny, on left,
also played in our band, The Forces of

Sound

Joe
and
750 lb
Bombs

Stars and Stripes Headline

Interesting Labels from area

Pictures from Ben McCorkle

Hahn Housing

Some of my Pictures

and Other Things

Orders to report for

physical

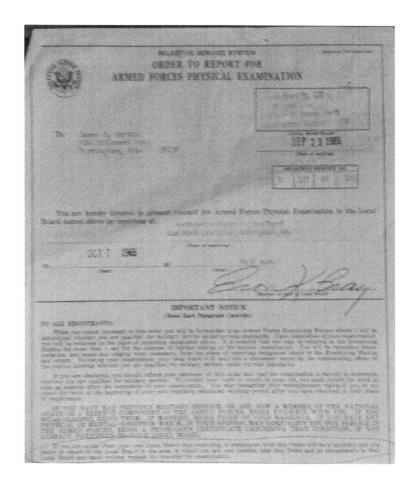

Orders to report to Hahn Air Base

DEPARTMENT OF THE AIR FORCE
HEADQUARTERS LOWRY TECHNICAL TRAINING CENTER (ATC)
LOWRY AIR FORCE BASE, COLORADO 80230

24 August 1966

SPECIAL ORDER
AA-658

ASSIGNMENT: Following airmen are relieved from pipeline stu, 3421 Stu
Sq, ATC, Lowry AFB, Colo; assigned unit indicated on PROJECT-USAFE-OCT-1010.
EDCSA: 15 Oct 66.
REPORTING DATA: DALVP. Report at MAC Passenger Svc Counter, McGuire AFB,
NJ 08641 approximately 10 Oct 66. Airmen are authorized to proceed on
delay en route prior to obtaining firm flt reservations in accordance with
para 3405, AFM 75-4. Orders will be indorsed at a later dt to include
firm flt reservations and AMD. Airmen will not report to APOE prior to
receiving firm flt reservations.
GENERAL INSTRUCTIONS: Authority: 6-AF-P6 for Sep 66. Comply with
AFM 75-4. New mailing address is: grade, full name, AFSN and unit of
assignment. Airmen are graduates of Class 03066, Weapons Mechanic, Crs
ABR46230-2 effective 3 Sep 66 and are awarded AFSC 46230 as prim. Properly
certified AF Form 286 will be inserted in Fld Personnel Records Gp prior
to departure from this base. Airmen are cleared for access to classified
material up to and including SECRET.
TRANSPORTATION: will proceed 4 Sep 66. PCS. TDN. 5773500 327 P577.02
1290 2161 2293 S503725 (object class code to be used as applicable).
CIC: 4 5 748 5776 503725 2131 2221. Hold baggage will be shipped in
accordance with AFM 75-4. Travel by military aircraft is authorized.
Prior to departure from this base, airmen will report to Traffic Management
Branch, Bldg 349, to obtain DD Form 1482, MAC Transportation Authorization.
Travel to port by POC with 6 days travel time authorized. If POC is not
used, travel time will be computed per para 1022, chap 1, AFM 39-11.
In the event of limited war or mobilization, you will proceed as scheduled.
In the event of general war or if the CONUS is attacked by a foreign
military force while you are en route to the port, you will report to the
nearest active AF installation as soon as possible.

LINE NO   LEAVE ADDRESS
350 Munitions Maintenance Sq, USAFE, APO New York 09109.
A3C DARRELL M BELL, AF14934920   JX5376-D-2BA   4058 Greenoak Dr, Donaville,
Ga
A3C FREDERICK C KUESTER JR, AF15768056   JX5377-D-2BA   4811 Subrenda Drive,
Sandston, Va
A3C RONALD D MORRIS, AF14950841   JX5378-D-2BA   203 Gregg St, High Point, NC
A3C JAMES E MARTIN, AF14931480   JX5379-D-2BA   924 Hillcrest Ave, Birmingham,
Ala

Me as a young troop at Hahn

Me (on right) with Mike, and Stu in barracks

room

PICTURE

OUTSIDE SHOP

CONCLUSION

Hahn Air Base! To the average reader these words mean absolutely nothing. However, to those of us who had the pleasure and good fortune to spend a short part of our lives at this wonderful little place in western Germany, the very words conjure up a whole host of memories. For many of us, these short years were while we were young and were forming that which was to be the beginning of our adult lives. Some of us (myself included) look at these years as some of the most valuable years of our life. Not only because it was a new experience for us to enjoy another part of this wonderful world, but it was a time when we learned so many of the life changing values we would learn to value from that time forward even to this present day. It was a time when we "grew up."

I for one am, <u>and will forever be</u> thankful that things turned out as they did so many years ago. Arriving in Germany is something that I remember well. It is that which I often reflect upon as one of a very few milestones in my life that I would not exchange for anything.

In the preceding pages many have shared testimonials, pictures, etc., of what their time at this wonderful little place meant to them. I would like to extend a huge "THANK YOU!" to all who participated. I am sure that there are possibly some that I may have overlooked. If this is the case, I certainly did not do so intentionally. Please accept my apology if this is the case!

As earlier stated, many of the entries are very similar. In fact, some are almost identical. This proves to me that many of us found enjoyment in many of the same things. Likewise, we found some of the same things unpleasant as well.

I trust that as you read these pages and reflect on the pictures that you will be reminded anew of what we were blessed to have experienced. If you get a small fraction of the satisfaction in reading what I received in writing/compiling then perhaps it will not have been in vain.

260

Made in the USA
Lexington, KY
19 April 2016